SPECTRUM®

Spelling

Grade 4

Published by Spectrum®
an imprint of Carson Dellosa Education
Greensboro, NC

Spectrum®
An imprint of Carson Dellosa Education
P.O. Box 35665
Greensboro, NC 27425 USA

Printed in the USA • All rights reserved.

ISBN 978-1-4838-1177-2

02-307207784

Table of Contents Grade 4

Table of Contents, continued

Pronunciation Key and Sample Words

The short **a** sound: b**a**g, d**a**d
The short **i** sound: p**i**g, **i**s
The short **o** sound: p**o**t, b**o**x
The short **u** sound: s**u**n, t**u**b
The short **e** sound: b**e**d, h**e**n

The long **a** sound: l**a**ke, st**ay**, w**ai**t
The long **i** sound: l**i**ke, m**y**, n**igh**t
The long **o** sound: h**o**me, n**o**, sl**ow**, c**oa**t, v**o**te
The long **e** sound: m**e**, f**ee**t, **ea**t, luck**y**
The long **u** sound: f**ew**, v**iew**, f**u**se

The /ü/ sound: r**oo**m, wh**ose**, r**u**de, m**o**ve, d**u**ty
The /ů/ sound: p**u**t, l**oo**k
The /ou/ sound: **ou**t, n**ow**
The /oi/ sound: j**oy**, b**oi**l
The /ô/ sound: s**aw**, t**a**lk, s**o**ng

The /ə/ sound: happ**e**n, roy**a**l, cott**o**n
The /əl/ sound: ang**le**, litt**le**

The /är/ sound: j**ar**, p**ar**k
The /âr/ sound: h**air**, c**are**, b**ear**
The /ôr/ sound: f**or**t, m**ore**, s**our**ce
The /ûr/ sound: g**ir**l, h**ur**t, upp**er**, **ear**ly, w**or**ry

The /j/ sound: **j**oke, pa**g**e, bri**dg**e
The /k/ sound: **c**at, bla**ck**, **k**angaroo
The /s/ sound: **s**pi**c**e, hou**s**e, **c**ent, **sc**ent
The /z/ sound: **z**oo, u**s**e, no**s**e

The /kw/ sound: **qu**een
The /skw/ sound: **squ**eeze

The /th/ sound: **th**ing, wi**th**
The /wh/ sound: **wh**y, **wh**ite
The /sh/ sound: **sh**ut, **sh**ip
The /ch/ sound: **ch**ild, tea**ch**

Lesson 1 Words with the Short **a** and Short **e** Sounds

Say each word. Listen for the short **a** sound and the short **e** sound. Then, write the word.

Spelling Tip	The short **a** and short **e** sounds often come between two consonants. The symbol for the short **a** sound is /a/. The symbol for the short **e** sound is /e/.

Spelling Words

sandwich	Sandwich
blanket	Blanket
effort	Effort
package	Package
extra	Extra
traffic	Traffic
napkin	Napkin
panic	Panic
basket	Basket
address	Address
cabin	Cabin
banner	Banner
gather	Gather
salad	Salad
celery	Celery

Lesson 1 Words with the Short **a** and Short **e** Sounds

Words in Context
Write the missing spelling words.

Rest from the City

Challenge

Circle the other two-syllable words in the narrative with the /a/ and /e/ sounds.

Last weekend, my family stayed

at a ___Cabin___ in the woods. First, we all had to make an

___Effort___ to ___Gather___ up the things we needed to

take. We loaded all our bags and a large ___Package___ of supplies

into the car. As we left the busy streets of the city

crowded with ___Traffic___, we began to relax.

Once we got into the country, we started looking for

the ___Address___ of our cabin on the mailboxes

near the road. There was a moment of ___Panic___ when we

thought we were lost. Then, my dad saw the large red ___Banner___

with the name of our campground written on it. We had finally arrived.

After we unpacked our things, we decided to go on a picnic. My mom

packed a ___basket___ full of food and covered it with a large

___Napkin___. My brother and I found a shady spot and spread out

a ___Blanket___ to sit on. We each had a ham ___Sandwich___

with ___Celery___ lettuce and tomato. We also had a mixed fruit

___Salad___ and crisp stalks of ___extra___ spread with

peanut butter. After we ate, we took a walk through the woods.

Lesson 1 Words with the Short **a** and Short **e** Sounds

Fun with Words

Unscramble the letters to make spelling words. Then, unscramble the
letters that you circle to solve the riddle.

1. frictaf ___traffic___ R I Circle letters 2 and 6.

2. creyle ___Celery___ L Y Circle letters 3 and 6.

3. banic ___Cabin___ C Circle letter 1.

4. pankni ___napkin___ N Circle letter 1.

5. takbes ___Basket___ T Circle letter 6.

6. daserds ___Address___ R E Circle letters 4 and 5.

7. eakgcap ___package___ C Circle letter 3.

8. trofef ___effort___ R Circle letter 4.

What word in the dictionary is spelled incorrectly? ___Dictionary___

Words Across the Curriculum

Say each science word. Then, write the word.

1. cactus ___Cactus___   3. element _____

2. desert ___Desert___   4. predator _____

Write the missing science words.

A ___Desert___ is a hot, dry habitat that is home to many

plants and animals. The dominant type of plant in this habitat is the

___cactu___. A common ___predator___ that eats small

lizards and mice in this habitat is the rattlesnake. In the American Southwest,

the ___element___ silver is found under the layers of sand and rock.

Lesson 1 Words with the Short **a** and Short **e** Sounds

Words in Writing

Write a narrative about something you like to do with your family. Use at least four words from the box.

> We go camping,
> we put so much effort into
> package. That I was tired. The
> traffic was endless, I put
> extra clothes incase.

sandwich	package	napkin	address	gather	cactus	desert
blanket	extra	panic	cabin	salad	element	predator
effort	traffic	basket	banner	celery		

Misspelled Words

Read the narrative and circle the seven misspelled words. Then, write the words correctly on the lines below.

I like to help my dad gathar vegetables from the garden. I pull carrots and celary from the ground and put them in a baskit. I also pick tomatoes, peppers, and other vegetables to use in a saled or on a sandwitch. Taking care of a garden is hard work, but it's worth the exra effert.

gather   celery   basket   salad

sandwich   extra   effort

NAME _____

Lesson 2 Words with the Short **i**, **o**, and **u** Sounds

Say each word. Listen for the short **i**, **o**, and **u** sounds. Then, write the word.

Spelling Tip	The short **i**, **o**, and **u** sounds often come between two consonants. The symbol for the short **i** sound is /i/. The symbol for the short **o** sound is /o/. The symbol for the short **u** sound is /u/.

Spelling Words

exit — _exit_

bottom — _bottom_

electric — _electric_

suggest — _suggest_

polish — _polish_

until — _until_

river — _river_

closet — _closet_

disappointed — _disappointed_

inspect — _inspect_

possible — _possible_

distance — _distance_

umbrella — _umbrella_

window — _window_

finish — _finish_

Lesson 2 Words with the Short **i**, **o**, and **u** Sounds

Words in Context

Write the missing spelling words.

No Escape

Challenge

Circle the other two-syllable words in the story with the /i/, /o/, and /u/ sounds.

I was planning to meet my

friends at the park by the ___swings___. Just as I was trying to make a

quick ___walk___ from the house, my mother appeared before me.

"Have you forgotten what I told you?" she asked. "You're not to go

anywhere ___until___ you tidy up your room," she said, wagging

her finger at me. "I ___say___ that you get it done now."

My heart sank, and I felt ___like___. I knew it wasn't

___going___ to invent any excuses. I slowly

trudged back to my room.

"I'll be ready to _____ your room

when you _____ with it," I heard my

mother call out from a _____.

I decided to surprise her by cleaning my room from top

to _____. I put my _____ and all my clothes

away neatly in the _____. I dusted the furniture and rubbed

_____ on it. I ran the _____ vacuum cleaner.

I even washed the _____ and shined the mirror. Finally, my

room was spotless. My mother was going to be very impressed!

NAME _____

Lesson 2 Words with the Short **i**, **o**, and **u** Sounds

Fun with Words

Alliteration is when a group of words have the same beginning sound. Use alliteration to write the spelling word that fits each sentence.

1. Clare cleaned her cluttered _____.

2. Will we wash the _____ with water?

3. We huddled under our umbrella _____ our uncle rescued us.

4. Ray rigged a rickety raft to ride the rapidly rising _____.

5. Fred forgot to _____ feeding the fifty fish he found.

6. Eleven excited elephants escaped from the _____.

7. I'll _____ the inside of the Inuit igloo.

8. Dozens of dentists' drills droned in the _____.

9. Ben built a box in the _____ of Bob's boat.

Words Across the Curriculum

Say each math word. Then, write the word.

1. multiple _____   3. intersect _____

2. prism _____   4. column _____

Write the math word that completes each sentence.

1. A _____ of data in a table is read from top to bottom.

2. Perpendicular lines _____ one another.

3. The number 16 is a _____ of 4.

4. A _____ is a solid shape that separates the colors of white light.

Lesson 2 Words with the Short i, o, and u Sounds

Words in Writing

Write a description of a chore that you do at home. Use at least two words from the box.

I fill yp water bottle.
and set up meals.

exit	suggest	river	possible	window	intersect	column
bottom	polish	closet	distance	finish	prism	
electric	until	inspect	umbrella	multiple	disappointed	

Dictionary Practice

Write the words from the box in the groups where they belong. Some words belong in more than one group.

/i/ Sound

Exit   electric   disappointed
River   Distance
Possible   finish
Window   prism
intersect   inspect

/o/ Sound

~~column~~
bottom
closet
multiple
collum

/u/ Sound

Suggest
~~column~~ mulitiple
polish
until
umbrella

Lesson 3 Words with **scr**, **squ**, **str**, and **thr**

Say each word. Listen to the beginning sounds. Then, write the word.

Spelling Tip	The letters **scr**, **squ**, **str**, and **thr** spell the beginning consonant sounds of some words.

Spelling Words

throne	throne
stretch	stretch
squirm	squirm
throw	threw
strap	strap
through	through
scream	scream
streak	streak
squeaky	squeaky
strength	strength
thrill	thrill
scrape	scrape
threat	threat
screw	screw
string	string

Lesson 3 Words with scr, squ, str, and thr

Words in Context

Write the missing spelling words.

Take a Deep Breath!

Challenge

Circle the other words with **scr**, **squ**, **str**, and **thr**.

Ride the Maximum Force roller coaster

for the ___thrill___ of a lifetime! The moment you squeeze into

a car and buckle your safety ___strap___, you'll begin to

___scream___ nervously in your seat. The metal

wheels of the cars will slowly ___scrape___ along

the rails as you move upward. On the first hill, the ride

will stop for a moment. You will feel like a king sitting on

his ___throne___ as you look out on the grounds

of the park that ___stretch___ out before you.

All of a sudden, the cars will jolt forward and nearly

___throw___ you out of your seat. The cars will ___streak___

along the track like lightning. As you seem to fly ___through___ the

air, you will hang onto the safety bar with all of your ___strength___.

Your throat will be so dry with fright that you won't even be able to

___scream___. But don't worry—there is no ___threat___ of

danger. Although the cables sound ___squeaky___ and are no

thicker than a ___string___, they're made of steel. Every latch,

cable, and ___screw___ on the ride is secure.

Lesson 3 Words with **scr**, **squ**, **str**, and **thr**

Fun with Words

Write the spelling word that rhymes with each underlined word.

1. It's quite a ___*thrill*___ to run down the <u>hill</u>.

2. I started to ___*scream*___ when I had a bad <u>dream</u>.

3. When you pull on the ___*string*___, the bell will <u>ring</u>.

4. I touched the <u>worm</u>, and it started to ___*squirm*___.

5. Why did you ___*scrape*___ the skin off the <u>grape</u>?

6. The queen was <u>alone</u> as she sat on her ___*throne*___.

7. Why did you ___*throw*___ the ball in the <u>snow</u>?

8. Please fasten the ___*strap*___ across your <u>lap</u>.

9. The boys used all their ___*strength*___ to run the last <u>length</u>.

10. The old stairs are <u>creaky</u>, and they're also ___*squeaky*___.

Words Across the Curriculum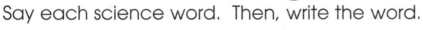

Say each science word. Then, write the word.

1. squid ___*Squid*___   3. squash ___*squash*___

2. straw ___*Straw*___   4. throat ___*throat*___

Write the science word that belongs with each group of words.

1. grass, wheat, hay, ___*grass, wheat, hay, straw*___

2. chin, ___*throat*___, neck, chest

3. potato, lettuce, tomato, ___*squash*___

4. octopus, ___*squid*___, jellyfish, sponge

Lesson 3 Words with scr, squ, str, and thr

Words in Writing

Write an ad for a ride or other attraction that you think is exciting. Use at least four words from the box.

Water Adventure park!

Throw the reuseable water balls, and ride the slides, WHAT A THRILL! Strech the slime, and pet the DOGS. Yo MAMA

throne	throw	scream	strength	threat	squid	straw
stretch	strap	streak	thrill	screw	squash	throat
squirm	through	squeaky	scrape	string		

Misspelled Words

Read the ad and circle the five misspelled words. Then, write the words correctly on the lines below.

Halloween is almost here, so be sure to visit the Haunted House. As you walk thruogh the dark, skweeky house, you will have one scary threll after another. You will experience spooky sounds and sights that will stretch your imagination. Try not to skream as the giant worms sqirm all around you!

_____   _____   _____

_____   _____

Lesson 4 Words with **ch** and **sh**

Say each word. Listen for the /ch/ and /sh/ sounds. Then, write the word.

Spelling Tip	The /ch/ sound is often spelled **ch**. The /sh/ sound is often spelled **sh**.

Spelling Words

bunch _____

cheese _____

hunch _____

shift _____

charge _____

perch _____

ranch _____

pinch _____

cherry _____

sheep _____

punch _____

cheap _____

shelter _____

chief _____

chance _____

Lesson 4 Words with **ch** and **sh**

Words in Context
Write the missing spelling words.

Challenge
Circle the other words with /ch/ and /sh/.

Agriculture in California

California is the ___most___

agricultural state. Crops are produced on a farm, while animals are raised

on a ___barn___. Orange, ___apples___, and peach

trees thrive in the hot days. The chilly nights give them a

___chanel___ to recover from the heat.

During the harvest, every fruit picker works a

long ___day___ from morning to evening.

Workers climb trees and _____

on the lower branches to reach the fruit.

Some workers _____ over

shrubs to pick blueberries and raspberries.

Others carefully pick each _____ of grapes from its vine.

Later, other workers take the grapes to a covered _____

and _____ the grapes from their stems. Some of the grapes

are made into juice and fruit _____.

Cows and _____ are also raised in California, so the

prices that the ranchers _____ for dairy products, including

milk and _____, are _____ there.

NAME _____

Lesson 4 Words with **ch** and **sh**

Fun with Words

Write the spelling word that answers the question "What am I?"

1. You need food, water and me to survive.
   What am I?   ~~shelter~~
                                                   ~~House~~
                                                   _____

2. Horses and cattle live on me. What am I?   _____Farm_____

3. I can mean a change or a time period of work.
   What am I?   _____

4. I can be positive, negative, or neutral. What am I? _____

5. I can be a group of bananas or grapes. What am I? _____

6. I am a leader of people or the main thing.
   What am I?   _____

7. I am a fruit and a popular flavor. What am I?   _____

8. You might like me best when I'm melted.
   What am I?   _____

Words Across the Curriculum

Say each language arts word. Then, write the word.

1. chapter _____   3. publish _____

2. research_____   4. English _____

Write the language arts word that fits each group of words.

1. edit, proofread, _____

2. paragraph, page, _____

3. French, Spanish, _____

4. references, sources, _____

Lesson 4 Words with **ch** and **sh**

Words in Writing

Write a short report about some goods that are produced in your state. Use at least four words from the box.

_____

_____

_____

_____

bunch	shift	ranch	sheep	shelter	chapter	research
cheese	charge	pinch	punch	chief	publish	English
hunch	perch	cherry	cheap	chance		

Misspelled Words

Read the paragraph from a report. Circle the five misspelled words. Then, write the words correctly on the lines below.

   I did some researsh about some foods and animals that are raised on farms in Wisconsin. Cows, hogs, and sheap make up most of the livestock raised in the state. A huge amount of milk, chease, and other dairy products are produced there, so these products are fairly cheep for the people of this state. I was surprised to find that Wisconsin farmers grow a large number of chery trees. However, apples are their chief fruit crop.

_____   _____   _____

_____   _____

Lesson 5 Silent Letters: Words with **gn**, **mb**, **tch**, and **wr**

Say each word. Listen to the sound of each consonant digraph and notice which letter is silent. Then, write the word. *Hello!*

Spelling Tip	The consonant digraphs **gn**, **mb**, **tch**, and **wr** each have a silent letter. In the consonant digraph **gn**, the **g** is silent. In the consonant digraph **mb**, the **b** is silent. In the consonant digraph **tch**, the **t** is silent. In the consonant blend **wr**, the **w** is silent.

Spelling Words

fetch	Fetch
wren	Wren
sketch	Sketch
design	design
wreck	Wreck
comb	Comb
twitch	Twitch
wrinkle	Wrinkle
ditch	Ditch
patch	Patch
limb	Limb
align	Align
wrench	Wrench
clutch	Clutch
snatch	Snatch

Lesson 5 Silent Letters: Words with **gn**, **mb**, **tch**, and **wr**

Words in Context
Write the missing spelling words.

Building a Birdhouse

Our art class had an interesting

assignment. We each had to ____BUILD____ a birdhouse. I began by

making a ____Plan____. I didn't have a ruler, so I used the edge of

my ____book____ to draw straight lines. When I was finished, I began

to ____get____ the materials I needed to build my birdhouse.

I took some wood, nails, and my drawing out to a tree in my

backyard. Then, I had to ____take____ my saw, a hammer, and a

____lot of wood____ all at once and carry them to the tree. There, I saw

my cat try to ____scratch____ my drawing. I knew that he was trying

to _____ my plan to build a safe place for birds. I chased

him into a _____ at the end of the yard. Then, I smoothed

out the _____ in my drawing. I carved a notch on a

_____ of the tree to mark the place for my birdhouse.

As I built it, I tried to _____ all the pieces of wood.

Now, a small brown _____ with a _____

of black on her throat often visits my birdhouse. She likes to watch my cat,

who can only stare back at her and _____ his whiskers. He

can't climb the tree.

Lesson 5 Silent Letters: Words with **gn**, **mb**, **tch**, and **wr**

Fun with Words

Write the spelling word that fits each sentence and has a consonant digraph that sounds the same as the underlined letters.

1. Will you please _____ the ma<u>tch</u>es from the hu<u>tch</u>?

2. Rachel will i<u>r</u>on the _____ in he<u>r</u> <u>r</u>ed d<u>r</u>ess.

3. Can you _____ a si<u>gn</u> to sell bolo<u>gn</u>a?

4. The ca<u>tch</u>er tried to _____ the ball before it rolled into the di<u>tch</u>.

5. The _____ is the <u>wr</u>ong tool to use to <u>r</u>epai<u>r</u> the <u>r</u>ake.

6. Please _____ the twi<u>ne</u> with the stem of the vi<u>ne</u>.

7. Did you atta<u>ch</u> a _____ on your scra<u>tch</u>?

8. The tiny b<u>r</u>own _____ pe<u>r</u>ched on the <u>wr</u>eath.

Words Across the Curriculum

Say each social studies word. Then, write the word.

1. wreath _____

2. tomb _____

3. lasagna _____

4. hitch _____

Write the social studies word that completes each sentence.

1. _____ is an Italian dish made with pasta, meat, and cheese.

2. Some people hang a _____ on the door during holidays.

3. Each pyramid in Egypt is the _____ of an ancient king or queen.

4. In the Old West, people used to _____ their horses to posts outside of stores.

Lesson 5 Silent Letters: Words with **gn**, **mb**, **tch**, and **wr**

Words in Writing

Write directions telling how to make or fix something. Use at least four words from the box.

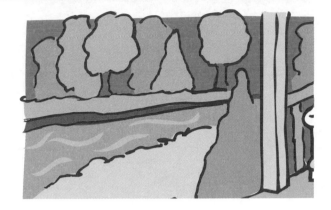

_____

_____

_____

_____

fetch	design	twitch	patch	wrench	wreath	tomb
wren	wreck	wrinkle	limb	clutch	lasagna	hitch
sketch	comb	ditch	align	snatch		

Dictionary Practice

Write the words from the box in alphabetical order. For some words, you will have to look at the third or fourth letter.

1. _____ 8. _____ 15. _____

2. _____ 9. _____ 16. _____

3. _____ 10. _____ 17. _____

4. _____ 11. _____ 18. _____

5. _____ 12. _____ 19. _____

6. _____ 13. _____

7. _____ 14. _____

Review Lessons 1–5

Write the spelling word that fits with each group of words.

1. lettuce, radish, carrot, _____

2. mattress, pillow, sheets, _____

3. peach, plum, apricot, _____

4. bolt, nut, nail, _____

5. rope, cord, twine, _____

6. sparrow, robin, finch, _____

7. milk, yogurt, butter, _____

8. soup, salad, chips, _____

9. brook, creek, stream, _____

10. hand, palm, thumb, _____

Write the spelling word that is a synonym for each word below.

11. shine _____

12. propose _____

13. excitement _____

14. ruin _____

15. flag _____

16. end _____

LESSONS 1–5 REVIEW

Review Lessons 1-5

Write the spelling word that means the same as each word below.

17. collect   _____

18. shriek   _____

19. toss   _____

20. grab   _____

21. branch   _____

22. wriggle   _____

Write the spelling word that completes each sentence.

23. Did you pack the food in the picnic _____?

24. The girls hung their coats in the _____.

25. The wheels of the old bike sound _____.

26. I taught my dog to _____ the newspaper.

27. I bought a _____ of ripe bananas.

28. Dad tightened the bolt on my bike with a _____.

29. I like the geometric _____ on that quilt.

30. Did you get _____ credit for your report?

Lesson 6 Words with the Long **a** Sound

Say each word. Listen for the long **a** sound. Then, write the word.

Spelling Tip	The long **a** sound can be spelled **a**, **a-consonant-e**, **ai**, **ay**, **ea**, and **eigh**. The symbol for the long **a** sound is /ā/.

Spelling Words

steak	steak
plain	plain
agent	agent
weight	weight
amaze	amaze
danger	danger
brain	Brain
bacon	BACON
brave	brave
escape	escape
paper	paper
neighbor	neighbor
trace	trace
cable	cable
behave	behave

Lesson 6 Words with the Long **a** Sound

Words in Context
Write the missing spelling words.

A Tall, Tall Tale

My dog Albert is incredible. The things

he can do would truly __amaze__ you. First of all, he uses his

__brain__ to think like a human. He doesn't __think__

like a dog at all. Albert likes to lay on the couch and watch cooking

programs on __our__ TV. He writes down the recipes on

notebook __page__. Last night, Albert invited our next-door

__neighbor__ over for dinner. Albert made grilled __cheese__,

baked potatoes, and a salad topped with cheese and __dressing__.

Albert is much more than a great cook. He is also a very

__smart__ dog who tracks criminals in his spare time. He once

helped a secret __detective__ catch an international thief. Albert

trailed the thief along a beach in Maine. The thief thought that Albert was

just a __plain__, ordinary dog. Thinking that he was in no

__danger__ of being caught, the thief broke into a beach house

and stole some jewels. He thought he would __escape__ from the

house without leaving a __trace__ of evidence. But Albert

threw all the __jewelry__ of his body at the thief and knocked him

down. Then, he used his cell phone to call for backup.

Lesson 6 Words with the Long a Sound

Fun with Words

Write the spelling word that completes each comparison.

1. *Chalk* is to *board* as *pen* is to _paper_.

2. *Inches* is to *height* as *pounds* is to _weight_.

3. *Public* is to *police* as *secret* is to _agent_.

4. *Battery* is to *cell phone* as _____ is to *television*.

5. *Breathe* is to *lungs* as *think* is to _____.

6. *Steak* is to *potatoes* as _____ is to *eggs*.

7. *Amazing* is to *unusual* as *ordinary* is to _____.

8. *Afraid* is to *scared* as *fearless* is to _____.

9. *Thrill* is to *boredom* as *safety* is to _____.

10. *Unfriendly* is to *enemy* as *friendly* is to _____.

Words Across the Curriculum

Say each math word. Then, write the word.

1. scale _____ 3. eighth _____

2. radius _____ 4. table _____

Write the math word that fits each group of words.

1. row, column, data, _____

2. area, diameter, circumference, _____

3. fifth, sixth, seventh, _____

4. balance, spring, weigh, _____

Lesson 6 Words with the Long **a** Sound

Words in Writing

Write a tall tale using made-up characters and exaggeration. Use at least four words from the box.

_____

_____

_____

_____

steak	weight	brain	escape	trace	scale	radius
plain	amaze	bacon	paper	cable	eighth	table
agent	danger	brave	neighbor	behave		

Dictionary Practice

Read the dictionary entries below. Then, read the example sentences. Write the part of speech and the number of the definition of the underlined words.

cable (kā′´bəl) *n.* **1.** a strong, thick cord. **2.** A bundle of wires enclosed in a protective covering and used to carry an electric current.
adj. **1.** Transmitted by cable TV. *v.* **1.** To transmit a message.

plain (plān) *adj.* **1.** Clearly seen or heard. **2.** Obvious; clearly understood. **3.** Without decoration. **4.** ordinary. *n.* **1.** An area of level land.

1. The judge made it plain that he did not agree.   _____

2. Suspension bridges are held up by steel cables.   _____

3. The woman wore a plain black raincoat.   _____

4. I like to watch comedy shows on cable TV.   _____

Lesson 7 Words with the Long e Sound

Say each word. Listen for the long **e** sound. Then, write the word.

Spelling Tip	The long **e** sound can be spelled **e**, **ee**, **ea**, **ie**, **y**, and **ey**. The symbol for the long **e** sound is /ē/.

Spelling Words

steam	steam
sweet	sweet
honey	honey
shield	sheild
treat	treat
screech	screech
least	least
beetle	beetle
reason	reason
breathe	breathe
field	feild
beast	beast
valley	valley
species	species
monkey	monkey

flower

Lesson 7 Words with the Long **e** Sound

Words in Context
Write the missing spelling words.

Challenge

Circle the other words in the report with the /ē/ sound.

Life in a Rain Forest

Tropical rain forests are the most diverse

ecosystems on Earth. More than half of all plant and animal

_____species_____ live in rain forests, which receive at _____least_____

50 inches of rain per year. Sometimes, the rain is so warm that water droplets

rise back into the air in the form of _____steam_____. Rain forest trees

give off oxygen that animals need to _____survive_____. The trees are

often clustered around a sloping river _____feild_____.

Most rain forest trees have leafy branches that grow only at the top.

These branches, called the canopy, _____shevel_____ the forest floor from

sunlight. From above, the canopy looks like a huge green _____.

All kinds of nuts and tropical fruits that are as _____ as

_____ grow in the canopy. For this _____,

most rain forest animals live in the canopy. There, it is common to see a

_____ or two swinging from branch to branch as they

_____ loudly at one another and search for fruit, nuts, or a

special _____, such as a cricket or a plump

_____. A strange _____, called a *sloth*, also

lives in the canopy.

NAME Feb 27 2022

Lesson 7 Words with the Long e Sound

Fun with Words

Circle the word in each sentence that is contained in the underlined spelling word. There can be more than one possible answer.

1. The impish <u>monkey</u> hid the key to his cage.

2. Let's eat a cookie for a <u>treat</u>.

3. The air that we <u>breathe</u> contains oxygen.

4. One swarm of bees can produce a lot of <u>honey</u>.

5. The driver needs to take at <u>least</u> one more turn before he heads east.

6. A team of scientists designed a new <u>steam</u> engine.

7. The student had a good <u>reason</u> for being late.

8. A black <u>beetle</u> is nibbling on the beet.

9. We like to eat <u>sweet</u> berries.

10. At the end of the alley, you can see the distant <u>valley</u>.

Words Across the Curriculum

Say each math word. Then, write the word.

1. mean Mean
2. degree degree
3. capacity Capacity
4. median Median

Write each math word next to its definition.

1. a unit used to measure temperature degree

2. the middle number in a group of numbers arranged from least to greatest Median

3. the amount of liquid that a container can hold Capacity

4. the average of a group of numbers Mean

Lesson 7 Words with the Long **e** Sound

Words in Writing YOU ROCK *Jaguar*

Write a short report about a rain forest animal. Use at least four words from the box.

The jaguar is a wild beast. It is a species of cat. In some regions jaguars eat a monkey or two. Jaguars are endangered. The reason is habitat loss.

steam	shield	least	breathe	valley	mean	degree
reason	treat	beetle	field	species	capacity	median
honey	screech	sweet	beast	monkey		

Misspelled Words

Read the paragraph. Circle the six misspelled words. Then, write the words correctly on the lines below.

Several different speces of monkeys live in tropical rain forests. Most rain forest monkeys are very social, like humans. They chatter with one another and screach loudly to warn other monkeys when a dangerous beest is nearby. Monkeys eat leaves, sweate fruits, flowers, seeds, and insects. A favorite treat of some monkeys is fresh honee or a plump beatle.

species   screech   beast

sweet   honey   beatle

Lesson 8 Words with the Long i Sound

Say each word. Listen for the long **i** sound. Then, write the word.

Spelling Tip	The long **i** sound can be spelled **i**, **i-consonant-e**, **igh**, and **y**. The symbol for the long **i** sound is /ī/.

Spelling Words

price	price
mild	mild
supply	supply
fight	fight
invite	invite
surprise	surpise
private	private
divide	divide
slight	slight
lightning	lightning
quite	quite
bicycle	bicycle
decide	decide
library	libray
drive	drive.

Lesson 8 Words with the Long i Sound

Words in Context

Write the missing spelling words.

It's a Party!

Dear Mike,

I'm writing to ___inform___ you to a ___invite___ party

for Casey. The party is next Saturday at Highland Park, which is right next to

the public ___indoor pool___. The weather

should be sunny and ___bright___, with

only a ___slight___ chance of rain and

___snow___. Kristi and I reserved the

___invi___ shelter near the pond. The party starts at five o'clock.

We will have a large _____ of food and soda. After we eat,

we can _____ into two teams and play baseball. I bought

_____ a few water balloons for a very low _____,

so we can also have a water-balloon _____. We can

_____ later what other games to play.

I hope you can come to the party. I think it will be really exciting! You

could ride your _____ to my house, and then my dad can

_____ us both to the park. Let me know soon.

Your friend,
Robbie

Lesson 8 Words with the Long i Sound

Fun with Words

Write the spelling word that completes each quote.

1. "Life is like riding a _____. You don't fall off unless you stop pedaling." –Claude Pepper

2. "When elephants _____, it is the grass that suffers." –African proverb

3. "If you must play, _____ upon three things at the start: the rules of the game, the stakes, and the quitting time." –Chinese proverb

4. "The public _____ is where place and possibility meet." –Stuart Dybek

5. "_____ and rule, unite and lead." –Johann Wolfgang von Goethe

6. "When you reach for the stars you may not _____ get one, but you won't come up with a handful of mud either." –Leo Burnett

Words Across the Curriculum

Say each science word. Then, write the word.

1. tide _____   3. hydrogen _____

2. biome _____   4. vitamin _____

Write the science word that completes each sentence.

1. The Sun is made up of mostly helium and _____ .

2. A _____ is a chemical compound that human bodies need.

3. A _____ is the rise and fall of surface water in the ocean.

4. A desert is a _____ that receives very little rain.

Lesson 8 Words with the Long i Sound

Words in Writing

Write a letter to a friend. Use at least four words from the box.

Dear, _____
Safa... SURPRISE
I'm so happy that you are
coming to my house. We can have
a slumber Party, pillow fight. Also, A
private Fort, like a mini biome.
_____

price	fight ✓	private ✓	lightning	decide	tide	biome ✓
mild	invite	divide	quite	library	hydrogen	vitamin
supply	surprise	slight	bicycle	drive		

Dictionary Practice

Divide the words below into syllables using hyphens. Use a dictionary if you need help.

1. invite _____
2. biome _____
3. supply _____
4. divide _____
5. private _____

6. hydrogen _____
7. lightning _____
8. surprise _____
9. library _____
10. bicycle _____

Lesson 9 Words with the Long o Sound

Say each word. Listen for the long **o** sound. Then, write the word.

Spelling Tip	The long **o** sound can be spelled **o**, **o-consonant-e**, **oa**, **ough**, and **ow**. The symbol for the long **o** sound is /ō/.

Spelling Words

over	Over
broke	Broke
motion	Motion
below	Below
choke	Stolen
stolen	Choke
noble	Noble
moment	Moment
swallow	Swallow
notice	Notice
spoke	Spoke
croak	Croak
propose	Propose
hollow	Hollow
although	Although

Lesson 9 Words with the Long o Sound

Words in Context

Write the missing spelling words.

Challenge

Circle the other words in the fable with the /ō/ sound.

The Fox and the Crow

A black crow sat on a limb of a

_____ tree. He was holding a piece of

cheese in his beak. The crow did not _____

the cheese. Instead, he held it in his beak so that the fox

sitting _____ the tree would

_____ it. The fox stared up at the crow for

a _____. Then, he _____

the silence.

"My, what a handsome and _____ bird you are," said

the sly fox. "Too bad your voice is just an ugly _____ ,

The crow became very angry. _____ he tried to

_____ back his words, he couldn't remain quiet.

"That's not true! I have a beautiful voice," the crow boasted.

As soon as he _____, the cheese fell from his beak. With

a single quick _____, the fox grabbed the cheese. The crow

groaned in despair as he watched the fox dine on the

_____ cheese.

"Thank you," said the fox, running his tongue _____ his

lips. "May I _____ a word of advice? Eating is more

important than pride."

Lesson 9 Words with the Long o Sound

Fun with Words

Sayings are common figures of speech that people use over and over again. Write the spelling word that completes each saying.

1. This is the straw that _____ the camel's back.

2. There's no point crying _____ spilled milk.

3. I decided to go shopping on the spur of the _____.

4. I was so sad that I had to _____ back my tears.

5. The lion is a _____ beast that's known as the king of the jungle.

6. We couldn't understand her, because she _____ in riddles.

7. That insult was really hard to _____.

8. _____ the thief looks honest, he lies like a rug.

Words Across the Curriculum

Say each science word. Then, write the word.

1. motor _____   **3.** rotate _____

2. ocean _____   **4.** proton _____

Write the science word that completes each sentence.

1. It takes Earth 24 hours to _____ on its axis.

2. An electric _____ changes electricity into mechanical energy.

3. The Pacific is the largest _____ on Earth.

4. A _____ has a positive charge.

Lesson 9 Words with the Long o Sound

Words in Writing

A fable is a short story that teaches a lesson about life. It includes a sentence or two at the end that tells what the lesson is. Write an existing fable in your own words, or make up a new one. Use at least four words from the box.

_____

_____

_____

_____

over	below	noble	notice	propose	motor	ocean
broke	choke	moment	spoke	hollow	rotate	proton
motion	stolen	swallow	croak	although		

Misspelled Words

Read the first paragraph of the fable. Circle the five misspelled words. Then, write the words correctly on the lines below.

A town mouse invited his country cousin over for dinner. The two mice were enjoying the scraps left on the dining table from a noable feast. They didn't noetice the mosion of the hungry cat entering the room, although they did hear a most frightening noise: a sound like the purring of a motore. The two mice froze and looked into the darkness beloe the table.

_____   _____   _____

_____   _____

Lesson 10 Words with the Long **u** and /ü/ Sounds

Say each word. Listen for the long **u** and /ü/ sound. Then, write the word.

> **Spelling Tip**
>
> The long **u** sound can be spelled **o-consonant-e**, **u**, **ue**, **iew**, **u-consonant-e**. The symbol for the long **u** sound is /ū/. The **oo** sound can be spelled **ew**, **u-consonant-e**, **oo**, and **ue**. The symbol for the /oo/ sound is /ü/.

Spelling Words

proof _____

duty _____

stew _____

issue _____

review _____

smooth _____

value _____

whose _____

troop _____

truce _____

regular _____

include _____

argue _____

usually _____

continue _____

Lesson 10 Words with the Long **u** and /ü/ Sounds

Words in Context

Write the missing spelling words.

Challenge

Circle the other words with the /ū/ or /ü/ sounds.

Please Join Our Group

Would you like to join a group of fun people? If so, we would like to ___recriut___ you as a member of our scouting ___program___. Our ___monthly___ meetings are on the first Tuesday of each month.

At our meetings, we _____ make plans for future activities. We also collect dues, which we use to pay for our activities. We _____ any other _____ that scout members want to discuss. We try not to _____ about these matters or lose our tempers. Instead, we talk calmly and try to _____ out any disagreements. We truly _____ every person's opinion. If we can't agree on something, we call a _____. Then, we _____ the discussion at the next meeting.

Our scouts have a strong sense of _____ to our community. This year, we had a yard sale to raise money for a family _____ house was damaged by a fire. We also made a huge batch of beef _____ for the homeless center. These activities are _____ of our commitment to our community.

Lesson 10 Words with the Long **u** and /ü/ Sounds

Fun with Words

Unscramble the letters to make spelling words. Then, unscramble the letters that you circle to solve the riddle.

1. grealru _____ Circle letter 5.

2. sweho _____ Circle letter 5.

3. dunlice _____ Circle letter 3.

4. wivere _____ Circle letter 4.

5. gerua _____ Circle letter 5.

6. shomot _____ Circle letter 1.

7. notunice _____ Circle letter 3.

What is so fragile that even saying its name can break it? _____

Words Across the Curriculum

Say each art word. Then, write the word.

1. music _____   **3.** flute _____

2. unity _____   **4.** statue _____

Write the art word that fits with each group of words.

1. variety, harmony, balance, _____

2. piano, trumpet, guitar, _____

3. tune, melody, song, _____

4. painting, drawing, pottery, _____

Lesson 10 Words with the Long **u** and /ü/ Sounds

Words in Writing

Write a flyer that persuades people to join a club or other group. Use at least four words from the box.

_____

_____

_____

_____

_____

_____

_____

proof	issue	value	truce	argue	music	unity
duty	review	whose	regular	usually	flute	statue
stew	smooth	troop	include	continue		

Dictionary Practice

Write the number of syllables in each word below.

1. issue _____

2. unity _____

3. smooth _____

4. continue _____

5. duty _____

6. regular _____

7. statue _____

8. include _____

9. review _____

10. usually _____

Review Lessons 6–10

Write the spelling word that is an antonym of each word below.

1. safety   _____

2. unite   _____

3. solid   _____

4. above   _____

5. public   _____

6. greatest   _____

7. sour   _____

8. rarely   _____

9. fixed   _____

10. rough   _____

11. bought   _____

Write the spelling word that belongs with each group of words.

12. juice, eggs, toast, _____

13. meadow, pasture, grassland, _____

14. skateboard, wagon, scooter, _____

15. string, cord, rope, _____

16. offer, suggest, advise, _____

Review Lessons 6–10

Write the spelling word that is a synonym of each word below.

17. simple _____

18. movement _____

19. evidence _____

20. protect _____

21. purpose _____

22. cost _____

23. very _____

24. battle _____

Write the spelling word that rhymes with each pair of words below.

25. beach, teach, _____

26. scoop, group, _____

27. lose, choose, _____

28. wake, break, _____

29. chunky, junky, _____

30. rally, tally, _____

31. dream, cream, _____

32. money, funny, _____

Lesson 11 Words with the /ôr/ Sound

Say each word. Listen for the /ôr/ sound. Then, write the word.

Spelling Tip	The /ôr/ sound can be spelled **or**, **ore**, and **our**.

Spelling Words

port _____

force _____

source _____

support _____

chore _____

report _____

before _____

fort _____

course _____

order _____

explore _____

record _____

border _____

landform _____

history _____

Lesson 11 Words with the /ôr/ Sound

Words in Context
Write the missing spelling words.

A Famous Expedition

In 1804, Merriwether Lewis and William

Clark began a famous journey in American _____. By the

_____ of President Thomas Jefferson, they left St. Louis to

_____ the western United States. The year _____,

the president had paid the French so Americans could use the territory.

The territory included the _____ city of New Orleans. It

extended the western _____ of the United States from the

Mississippi River to the Pacific Ocean. Lewis and Clark began their journey

aboard a keelboat on the Missouri River and followed the river to its

_____. They took about 45 men with them for protection

and _____. They also built a _____. As the

_____ of the river carried them along, Clark spent most of

his time charting their _____ and making maps.

Lewis's main _____ was to _____ his

observations of each new animal, plant, and _____ that he

saw. The men survived because Native Americans helped them. Lewis

would later _____ this information to the president.

Challenge

Circle the other words in the report with the /ôr/ sound.

Lesson 11 Words with the /ôr/ Sound

Fun with Words

Use the letters of each spelling word below to make at least three four-letter words.

1. landform _____

2. course _____

3. support _____

4. record _____

5. before _____

6. history _____

7. Two of the spelling words have all of the same letters. The only difference is that two of the letters are reversed. Which words are they?

_____

Words Across the Curriculum

Say each social studies word. Then, write the word.

1. court _____   3. uniform _____

2. afford _____   4. export _____

Write the social studies word that completes each sentence.

1. The United States and Canada _____ many goods.

2. If you can't _____ to buy something you want right away, you can wait until you save enough money.

3. A trial is held in a _____.

4. A police officer wears a _____ so that people can identify him or her.

Lesson 11 Words with the /ôr/ Sound

Words in Writing

If you could live in any place at any time in history, where would it be? Write about this time and place. Use at least four words from the box.

_____

_____

_____

_____

_____

port	support	before	order	border	court	afford
force	chore	fort	explore	landform	uniform	export
source	report	course	record	history		

Misspelled Words

Read the description. Circle the five misspelled words. Then, write the words correctly on the lines below.

    If I could go back in history, I'd like to live about 100 years ago. I would live on a tropical island in the days befor any people lived there. I would explour every beach and landforme. I'd keep a journal to recorde all the interesting things I saw. I would also sail on a boat beyond the boreder of the land.

_____ _____ _____

_____ _____

Lesson 12 Words with the /ûr/ Sound

Say each word. Listen for the /ûr/ sound. Then, write the word.

Spelling Tip	The /ûr/ sound can be spelled **er**, **ear**, **ir**, **or**, and **ur**.

Spelling Words

curve _____

heard _____

worry _____

further _____

perfect _____

worth _____

return _____

shirt _____

hurry _____

surge _____

expert _____

search _____

purpose _____

certain _____

thirsty _____

Lesson 12 Words with the /ûr/ Sound

Words in Context

Write the missing spelling words.

Earning a Comeback

This morning was my first soccer game of the season, but I overslept. I had to _____ through my closet for my gear and _____ to the field as quickly as I could. I was _____ that I'd be late, but it turned out that there was no need to _____. The game hadn't started yet.

I took off my _____ and put on my jersey. Then, I _____ the referee blow his whistle, so I joined my team on the field. During the first half of the game, the opposing team dominated us. Our players pursued the ball without any real _____. At halftime, we were discouraged, hot, and _____. We did not think it was _____ the effort to _____ to the field to face _____ embarrassment.

Somehow, our coach managed to encourage us. He is an _____ at making us focus on doing our best. We came back in the second half with a _____ of energy. With the score tied near the end of the game, our best striker scored a _____ goal. He faked around his defender and was able to _____ the ball into the top of the goal.

Lesson 12 Words with the /ûr/ Sound

Fun with Words

Use the clues to complete the puzzle with spelling words.

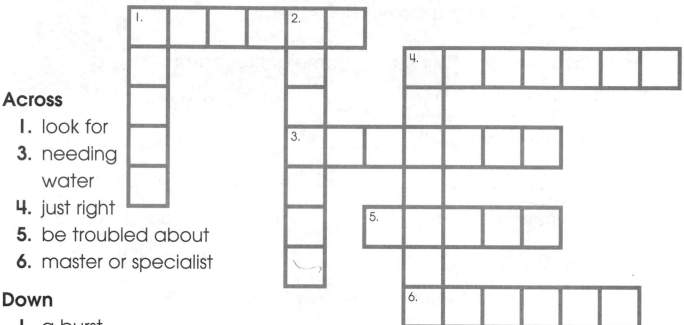

Across

1. look for
3. needing water
4. just right
5. be troubled about
6. master or specialist

Down

1. a burst
2. sure
4. reason

Words Across the Curriculum

Say each science word. Then, write the word.

1. germ _____

2. Earth _____

3. current _____

4. pearl _____

Write the science word that completes each sentence.

1. A _____ can flow deep beneath the surface of the ocean.

2. The moon revolves around _____.

3. A _____ can be seen only with a microscope.

4. A _____ is a gem formed inside of an oyster.

Lesson 12 Words with the /ûr/ Sound

Words in Writing

Describe a sports event that you watched or participated in. Use at least four words from the box.

_____

_____

_____

_____

curve	further	return	surge	purpose	germ	Earth
heard	perfect	shirt	expert	certain	current	pearl
worry	worth	hurry	search	thirsty		

Dictionary Practice

Circle the correct pronunciation for the words below. Use a dictionary if you need help.

1. pearl   perl   pûrl   pûr el

2. curve   cûrve   kûrv   kerv

3. perfect   pûrf´ ect   per´ fek   pûr´ fikt

4. further   fur´ thur   fûr´ ther   ferth´ er

5. thirsty   thûrs´ tī   thīr´ stē   thûr´ ste

6. heard   herd   hûred   hûrd

7. surge   surg   cûrj   sûrj

Lesson 13 Words with the /ə/ Sound

Say each word. Listen for the /ə/ sound in the final syllable. Then, write the word.

Spelling Tip	The /ə/ sound can be spelled **a**, **e**, and **o**. The /ə/ sound is common in unstressed syllables.

Spelling Words

model   _____

royal   _____

cotton   _____

central   _____

custom   _____

flavor   _____

towel   _____

happen   _____

local   _____

lemon   _____

jewel   _____

capital   _____

travel   _____

normal   _____

natural   _____

Lesson 13 Words with the /ə/ Sound

Words in Context

Write the missing spelling words.

An Unusual Shopping Trip

If you ever _____ to _____ to Egypt, be

sure to visit the famous marketplaces in Cairo, the _____

city. The marketplaces have a mix of modern and ancient things,

including a _____ palace in one! Inside the

_____ part of the marketplace, there is often a maze of

shops that sell all kinds of things. You can find a _____ of a

famous building or a beautiful _____. You also can find a

carpet, _____, or other piece of

cloth made of Egypt's famous, high-quality

_____.

Outside the marketplaces, many

_____ farmers set up stalls with

fruits, vegetables, and other _____ products, which they

unload each day from their wagons. You can almost taste the bitter

_____ of a juicy _____ or a delicious spice. It

is _____ to find amazing things in the marketplaces!

Lesson 13 Words with the /ə/ Sound

Fun with Words

The letters in one or two words in each sentence can be rearranged to form a spelling word. Circle the words and then rearrange the letters to make the spelling word.

1. I will not sit on that cot! _____

2. The lunar spaceship landed on the moon at noon. _____

3. My dad lent his car to his barber. _____

4. Would you like a ripe, juicy melon? _____

5. Did you lay your gloves down or did you lose them? _____

6. We bought a lot of apples today. _____

7. The old man gave me some wise advice. _____

8. I did a sum while I lay on the cot. _____

Words Across the Curriculum

Say each science word. Then, write the word.

1. metal _____   3. carbon _____

2. organ _____   4. water _____

Write the science word that completes each sentence.

1. The _____ that pumps blood in the body is the heart.

2. _____ is a mixture of hydrogen and oxygen.

3. A _____ is usually a hard, solid, shiny substance.

4. _____ is an element found in the remains of all living things.

Lesson 13 Words with the /ə/ Sound

Words in Writing

Describe a tradition in your family.
Use at least four words from the box.

_____

_____

_____

_____

_____

_____

_____

model	central	towel	lemon	travel	metal	organ
royal	custom	happen	jewel	normal	carbon	water
cotton	capital	local	flavor	natural		

Misspelled Words

Read the description. Circle the five misspelled words. Then, write the words correctly on the lines below.

My grandmother is from the centrel part of Greece. She isn't able to traval there very often, but she still follows many Greek customs. She makes Greek food using naturel ingredients that she buys from a local farm market. She uses lemen juice to add a tart flaver to many of the dishes she makes.

_____   _____   _____

_____   _____

Review Lessons 11–13

Write the spelling word that is an antonym of each word below.

1. closer _____

2. after _____

3. unsure _____

4. game _____

5. unusual _____

6. leave _____

Write the spelling word that is a synonym of each word below.

7. goal _____

8. tradition _____

9. command _____

10. arch _____

11. taste _____

12. occur _____

13. path _____

14. edge _____

15. value _____

Review Lessons 11–13

Write the spelling word that belongs with each group of words.

16. mountain, desert, volcano, _____

17. aching, tired, hungry, _____

18. pants, sweater, vest, _____

19. king, queen, prince, _____

20. orange, grapefruit, lime, _____

21. velvet, wool, silk, _____

22. diamond, ruby, emerald, _____

23. seek, hunt, pursue, _____

24. journey, trip, visit, _____

25. robe, washcloth, sponge, _____

26. inform, notify, broadcast _____

27. origin, root, beginning, _____

28. pro, master, specialist _____

29. help, aid, assistance, _____

30. power, strength, might, _____

Lesson 14 Possessive Nouns

Say each word. Notice how the order of the **s** and the apostrophe shows whether the word is singular or plural. Then, write the word.

Spelling Tip	**Possessive nouns** are words that show ownership. When a noun shows that one person or thing owns something, the noun ends with **'s**. Usually, when a noun shows that more than one person or thing owns something, the noun ends with **s'**.

Spelling Words

baby's   _____

mother's   _____

brothers'   _____

officer's   _____

friend's   _____

sister's   _____

children's   _____

family's   _____

everyone's   _____

hamster's   _____

friends'   _____

father's   _____

grandmothers'   _____

customers'   _____

families'   _____

Lesson 14 Possessive Nouns

Words in Context

Write the missing spelling words.

Everything Not Being Used Must Go!

This summer, the people on my block had a big yard sale. The sale was held in my _____ yard. This was my _____ idea. At first, she just wanted to get rid of my youngest _____ old dresses and coats. Then, she decided that both of my _____ old baseball equipment had to go, too. She began searching through _____ closets and drawers to see what she could get rid of. She even went through my _____ office to find things that he didn't use anymore.

My mother offered to help clear out some of her _____ houses, too. Soon, our yard was filled with other _____ old and unused items. There was a _____ crib, a _____ cage, an old police _____ uniform, and all kinds of _____ toys and clothes. My best _____ mother brought over a box full of both of her _____ old-fashioned dresses. When the sale was over, we had collected more than $200 of our _____ money.

Lesson 14 Possessive Nouns

Fun with Words

Write the spelling word that explains the relationship described in each sentence.

1. My mother's sons' bikes are my _____ bikes.

2. My parents' mothers' coats are my _____ coats.

3. My mother's daughter's desk is my _____ desk.

4. My grandfather's only son's car is my _____ car.

5. My buddy's mother is my _____ mother.

6. My aunt's only sister's dog is my _____ dog.

7. My parents' _____ toys are my brother's and sister's toys.

8. My parents' and their children's house is my _____ house.

Words Across the Curriculum

Say each art word. Then, write the word.

1. painters' _____   3. actors' _____

2. dancers' _____   4. artists' _____

Write the missing art words.

People enjoy many different kinds of _____ work. Some

people like to visit museums to see their favorite _____ works

of art. Some people enjoy going to a play to see the _____

performances. Others enjoy watching a group of _____

movements onstage.

Lesson 14 Possessive Nouns

Words in Writing

Write a short story about something funny or interesting that happened to you or members of your family. Use at least four words from the box.

_____

_____

_____

_____

baby's	friend's	everyone's	families'	actors'
mother's	sister's	hamster's	grandmothers'	dancers'
brothers'	children's	friends'	customers'	artists'
officer's	family's	father's	painters'	

Misspelled Words

Read the story. Circle the four possessive nouns that are used or spelled incorrectly. Then, write the correct possessive nouns.

I was taking care of my best friends' hamster while he went to his familys' cabin for a week. On the second morning, the hamsters' cage was empty. My oldest sister's cat was licking its paws in a corner of my room. I gasped and ran into my parents' bedroom. I couldn't understand why they were both laughing. Then, I saw the hamster curled up inside one of my fathers' slippers.

_____   _____

_____   _____

Lesson 15 Easily Misspelled Words

Say each word. Look for familiar and unfamiliar spelling patterns. Then, write the word.

Spelling Tip	Some words have unusual spellings. You have to remember how these words are spelled.

Spelling Words

person _____

sure _____

touch _____

tropical _____

young _____

island _____

built _____

against _____

different _____

palm _____

awhile _____

answer _____

mountain _____

remember _____

camera _____

Lesson 15 Easily Misspelled Words

Words in Context

Write the missing spelling words.

A Vacation in Paradise Awaits You

Would you like to relax for _____ on a quiet beach

without having another _____ in sight? If the

_____ to this question is yes, please plan to visit our beautiful

_____. You will be _____ to enjoy your stay.

You can lie in a hammock under a _____ tree as a cool

breeze blows gently _____ your skin. You can wade along

the shore and feel the warm _____ of the sparkling blue

ocean.

There are many _____ things to do here, whether you

are old or _____. You can hike up the stone steps that were

_____ into the slope of a _____ hundreds of

years ago. You also can take a walk through our _____ rain

forest. _____ to bring your _____ so you can

take pictures of the beautiful scenery.

Lesson 15 Easily Misspelled Words

Fun with Words

Alliteration is when a group of words have the same beginning sound. Use alliteration to write the spelling word that best fits each sentence.

1. She's _____ she saw sheep shivering in the shade.

2. Tourists tried to twist through the trails under the _____ trees.

3. Bill _____ a box with black and blue blocks.

4. You'll be _____ for years.

5. The members must _____ to meet at midnight.

6. Dino demands a _____ dish every day for dinner.

7. Ann acted _____ Aunt Alice's advice.

8. Ken's _____ captured a captivating shot of the calico cats.

9. We will wait _____ for warmer weather.

Words Across the Curriculum

Say each math word. Then, write the word.

1. height _____

2. symbol _____

3. cylinder _____

4. graph _____

Write the math word that completes each sentence.

1. A tube is shaped like a _____.

2. The volume of a rectangle is its length times its width times its

_____.

3. Ordered pairs can be plotted on a _____.

4. The _____ for cubic centimeters is cm³.

Lesson 15 Easily Misspelled Words

Words in Writing

Write an ad for a vacation spot that you would like to visit. Use at least four words from the box.

_____

_____

_____

_____

_____

_____

_____

person	tropical	built	palm	mountain	height	symbol
sure	young	against	awhile	remember	cylinder	graph
touch	island	different	answer	camera		

Dictionary Practice

Use hyphens to show where to divide each word into syllables. Use a dictionary if you need help.

1. camera _____

2. mountain _____

3. answer _____

4. cylinder _____

5. different _____

6. remember _____

7. measure _____

8. symbol _____

Lesson 16 Irregular Plurals

Say each pair of words. Notice how the spelling of the plural form is different from the singular form. Also notice that one word does not have a singular form. Then, write each plural word.

Spelling Tip	When a noun ends with **f** or **fe**, change the **f** or **fe** to **v** before adding **es**. A few nouns have plural forms that you have to remember.

Spelling Words

leaf	leaves	_____
calf	calves	_____
life	lives	_____
ox	oxen	_____
wife	wives	_____
half	halves	_____
mouse	mice	_____
wolf	wolves	_____
thief	thieves	_____
loaf	loaves	_____
goose	geese	_____
knife	knives	_____
shelf	shelves	_____
scarf	scarves	_____
themselves		_____

Lesson 16 Irregular Plurals

Words in Context

Write the missing spelling words.

The Story of Ali Baba

A popular Middle Eastern folktale tells the story of Ali Baba and the forty _____. Ali Baba found the robbers' secret cave hidden behind the _____ of some thick bushes. Ali Baba listened at the door of the cave. He knew that the robbers would attack him like a pack of _____ pouncing on a flock of _____ or a herd of helpless _____ if they found him there. He heard nothing but a few _____ nibbling on _____ of bread.

When Ali Baba entered the cave, he saw all kinds of treasures heaped upon _____ and tables. He saw piles of gold and valuable goods, such as ladies' _____ and sharp _____ with jeweled handles. Ali Baba loaded a few bags of treasure onto his _____.

Ali Baba and his brother Cassim got along well, but their _____ stirred up trouble. Cassim's wife thought that the brothers should split the treasure between _____ in two _____. Cassim went to the cave and took so much treasure that the robbers noticed it was missing. The _____ of the brothers were in danger.

Lesson 16 Irregular Plurals

Fun with Words

Write the spelling word that names things you might find in each place.

1. inside a
   library _____

2. in a kitchen
   drawer _____

3. on a
   branch _____

4. with
   cows _____

5. at a pond _____

6. with their
   husbands _____

7. around people's
   necks _____

8. in a
   bakery _____

9. in the
   mountains _____

10. in prison _____

Words Across the Curriculum

Say each pair of words. Notice how the spelling of the plural form is different from the singular form. Also notice that one word does not have a singular form. Then, write the plural word.

1. elf elves _____

2. woman women _____

3. child children _____

4. ourselves _____

Write the missing irregular plural nouns.

1. The _____ made sandcastles on the beach.

2. _____ are imaginary creatures who sometimes help humans.

3. We are going to the park by _____.

4. I love when the _____ change color in autumn.

Lesson 16 Irregular Plurals

Words in Writing

Write your own folktale or fable. Use at least four words from the box.

_____

_____

_____

_____

leaves	oxen	mice	loaves	shelves	elves	women
calves	wives	wolves	geese	scarves	children	ourselves
lives	halves	thieves	knives	themselves		

Misspelled Words

Read the fable. Circle the five misspelled words. Then, write the words correctly.

A group of mouses once roamed the kitchen of a farmhouse. They climbed up the shelfs and tables, eating crumbs from loafs of bread and pieces of cheese. When the master of the house bought a cat, they held a meeting among themselfs to see how they could outwit the cat.

"Let's tie a bell around the cat's neck," said a young mouse.

"That's easy to say," replied an older mouse. "But who among us will actually risk their lifes to become heroes?"

_____   _____   _____

_____   _____

Lesson 17 Words with the Final /əl/ Sound

Say each word. Listen to the final /əl/ sound. Then, write the word.

Spelling Tip	The /əl/ sound at the ends of words is often spelled **le**.

Spelling Words

settle _____

angle _____

title _____

bubble _____

trouble _____

sparkle _____

kettle _____

simple _____

scramble _____

terrible _____

puzzle _____

scribble _____

tremble _____

double _____

trickle _____

Lesson 17 Words with the Final /əl/ Sound

Words in Context
Write the missing spelling words.

Challenge

Circle the other words in the story with the final /əl/ sound spelled **le**.

The First National Park

Imagine you are watching a pool of water _____ in the sun. Suddenly, it begins to _____. The water looks like it is boiling as a _____ of steam rises from its surface. The ground begins to _____. You _____ to a safe place to watch. Suddenly, a huge jet of hot water shoots into the air at a right _____. You smile as you _____ down and enjoy the incredible sight.

What you saw is called a geyser. How they worked was once a _____ to people. However, scientists now know that the way they work is quite _____. They might make you _____ when they erupt, but don't worry! You can stay out of _____ by following each rule for safety there.

Lesson 17 Words with the Final /əl/ Sound

Fun with Words

Sayings are familiar phrases that have been used over and over again. Write the spelling word that completes each saying.

1. The truth is pure and _____.

2. This is a fine _____ of fish!

3. I need to _____ a score with you.

4. Her eyes _____ like diamonds.

5. I don't want to burst your _____, but . . .

6. I started to _____ like a leaf in the wind.

7. The money began to slowly _____ in.

8. The detective finally put together the pieces of the _____.

Words Across the Curriculum

Say each science word. Then, write the word.

1. ankle _____

2. muscle _____

3. cycle _____

4. particle _____

Write the science word that belongs with each group of words.

1. atom, molecule, _____

2. bone, tendon _____

3. water, life _____

4. knee, elbow _____

Lesson 17 Words with the Final /əl/ Sound

Words in Writing

Write notes about some things that you know about water. Use at least four words from the box.

_____

_____

_____

_____

settle	bubble	kettle	terrible	tremble	ankle	muscle
angle	trouble	simple	puzzle	double	cycle	particle
title	sparkle	scramble	scribble	trickle		

Misspelled Words

Read the notes about water. Circle the five misspelled words. Then, write the words correctly.

Water on Earth goes through a simple sycle.

There's more than doubele the amount of water in oceans than in lakes and rivers.

Particels of water from oceans rise and collect in clouds.

When rain falls to Earth, some water drops setle in puddles. Others trikle from tree branches down to the ground.

_____   _____   _____

_____   _____

Lesson 18 Homophones

Say each word. Notice the different spellings of the words that sound the same. Then, write each word.

Spelling Tip	**Homophones** are words that sound the same but have different spellings and meanings.

Spelling Words

close   _____

sight   _____

poor   _____

peek   _____

groan   _____

waste   _____

clothes   _____

miner   _____

pour   _____

site   _____

peak   _____

waist   _____

grown   _____

pore   _____

minor   _____

Lesson 18 Homophones

Words in Context

Write the missing spelling words.

San Francisco, 1849

I arrived in San Francisco in 1849 to become a

gold _____. I spent most of my

money to pay my fare on the ship, so now I was

_____. I didn't have a penny to _____. This, I

thought, was only a _____ problem. Soon, I'd be rich.

With the money I had left, I bought some food and work

_____ at a general store. I put them on and strapped my

belt around my _____ . As I paid for my goods, the store

clerk described how the city had _____ in the past year. I

reached behind me to _____ the door of the store and

began a new chapter of my life.

I started down the dusty trail with the _____ of a

mountain _____ looming before me. After a few days, I

found a good _____ to look for gold. With a loud

_____, I dropped my heavy pack. Sweat dripped from every

_____ of my skin. As I sat down by the creek bed and began

to _____ water over my head, I saw something sparkling in the

mud. I closed my eyes before I dared to take another _____.

Lesson 18 Homophones

Fun with Words

Write the spelling word that completes each quote.

1. "It's not the man who has too little that is _____; it's the man who always wants more." –Unknown

2. "Today I have _____ taller from walking with the trees." –Karle Wilson Baker

3. "_____ not, want not." –Unknown

4. "A person who is out of _____ is soon out of mind." –Unknown

5. "You can't judge a book by its cover or a man by his

_____." –Unknown

6. "Happiness is a perfume which you cannot _____ on someone without getting some on yourself." –Ralph Waldo Emerson

Words Across the Curriculum

Say each pair of words that sound the same. The underlined word is the science word. Look at the different spellings. Then, write the science word.

1. <u>scent</u>, sent _____   3. foul, <u>fowl</u> _____

2. beat, <u>beet</u> _____   4. <u>heel</u>, he'll _____

Write the science homophone that completes each sentence.

1. A _____ is a vegetable that grows underground.

2. The rounded, back part of a human foot is the _____.

3. Ducks and geese are both water _____.

4. The color and _____ of a flower attracts bees.

Lesson 18 Homophones

Words in Writing

Make up some wise sayings, or proverbs. Use at least four words from the box.

_____

_____

_____

_____

close	peek	clothes	site	grown	scent	beet
sight	groan	miner	peak	pore	fowl	heel
poor	waste	pour	waist	minor		

Dictionary Practice

Read the dictionary entries. Then, write the part of speech and the number of the definition for the underlined word in each sentence.

waste *n.* **1.** The act of using carelessly. **2.** A wild or deserted place with few or no living things. *v.* **1.** To use up or spend in a careless way. **2.** To destroy or ruin.

foul *adj.* **1.** Unpleasant or disgusting. **2.** Very bad; evil. *v.* **1.** To make dirty. **2.** To break a rule in sports, especially by unfairly touching another player.

1. The rotten bananas had a <u>foul</u> smell. _____

2. The invading army <u>wasted</u> everything in its path. _____

3. Watching that movie was a <u>waste</u> of time. _____

4. I got a free throw because a player on the other team <u>fouled</u> me.

_____

Review Lessons 14–18

Write the spelling word that is an antonym of each word.

1. same _____

2. rich _____

3. husbands _____

4. wonderful _____

5. forget _____

6. old _____

7. complex _____

8. open _____

9. question _____

10. for _____

Write the spelling word that belongs with each group of words.

11. eighths, fourths, thirds, _____

12. chicks, lambs, foals, _____

13. plates, forks, spoons, _____

14. hill, volcano, cliff, _____

15. point, line, side, _____

16. riddle, mystery, maze, _____

17. moan, shriek, cry, _____

18. twice, couple, pair, _____

Review Lessons 14–18

Write the spelling word that is a synonym of each word.

19. made _____

20. robbers _____

21. twinkle _____

22. dad's _____

23. shake _____

24. moms' _____

25. certain _____

26. name _____

Write the spelling word that completes each sentence.

27. The _____ crib was full of toys and blankets.

28. The autumn _____ are red and orange.

29. Are there many _____ trees on this island?

30. Mother likes to bake _____ of bread.

31. Do you have your _____ hat on?

32. _____ are members of the dog family.

Lesson 19 Words with the /j/ Sound

Say each word. Listen for the /j/ sound. Then, write each word.

Spelling Tip	The /j/ sound can be spelled **j**, **g**, or **dje**.

Spelling Words

bridge   _____

jazz   _____

image   _____

luggage   _____

jumble   _____

range   _____

message   _____

jockey   _____

manage   _____

gentle   _____

plunge   _____

cabbage   _____

lodge   _____

garbage   _____

dangerous   _____

Lesson 19 Words with the /j/ Sound

Words in Context
Write the missing spelling words.

What to Do?

Grown-ups always ask what I want to do when I grow up. There's such a large _____ of things to do that I haven't decided yet. I'd like to be a _____, but that would be very _____. Racehorses aren't known for being _____ animals. I'm afraid I'd fall off and _____ to the ground with my arms and legs all in a _____. I can just imagine the X-ray _____ of all the damaged bones in my body.

I wouldn't mind working in a ski _____. I could help the skiers take their _____ to their rooms and give them a _____ when someone wants to reach them. Or, I could work in the kitchen, chopping up _____ and other vegetables. I'd probably have to clean the whole kitchen and take out the _____, too. On second thought, if I worked in a ski resort, I'd want to _____ all the other workers. Or, I could be an engineer and design the longest _____ in the world. I could play in a _____ band at night.

Lesson 19 Words with the /j/ Sound

Fun with Words

Write the spelling word that answers each clue.

1. If you travel a lot, you have to lug me around.   _____

2. I come from ragtime and the blues.
   Bebop, rock, and hip-hop came from me.   _____

3. My job is racing, but I don't run.   _____

4. You see me when you look in a mirror.   _____

5. Nobody likes me; everyone always
   wants to get rid of me.   _____

6. I bring places together.   _____

7. I am the head of the garden.   _____

8. I shelter people in the woods and mountains.   _____

Words Across the Curriculum

Say each social studies word. Then, write the word.

1. jury   _____   3. badge   _____

2. reject   _____   4. justice   _____

Write the social studies word that completes each sentence.

1. A police officer wears a _____ to identify himself or herself.

2. The court system is meant to provide _____ for all citizens.

3. A judge can _____ evidence from a court.

4. A judge or a _____ can make a decision in a legal trial.

Lesson 19 Words with the /j/ Sound

Words in Writing

Describe a trip that you'd like to take. Use at least four words from the box.

_____

_____

_____

_____

_____

_____

bridge	luggage	message	gentle	dangerous	jury	reject
jazz	jumble	jockey	plunge	lodge	badge	justice
image	range	manage	cabbage	garbage		

Misspelled Words

Read the description. Circle the four misspelled words. Then, write the words correctly.

I'd like to stay at a ski lodje in the mountains. As soon as I got there, I'd take my luggadge to my room and put on my ski clothes. I'd leave a messaje for my parents that I would be on the slopes all day. I'd get my ski badge, ride the ski lift up a mountain, and plundge down the slope.

_____   _____

_____   _____

Lesson 20 Words with the /k/ Sound

Say each word. Listen for the /k/ sound. Then, write each word.

Spelling Tip	The /k/ sound can be spelled **c**, **k**, and **ck**.

Spelling Words

junk   _____

socket   _____

carpet   _____

kangaroo   _____

corner   _____

picnic   _____

ticket   _____

candle   _____

bucket   _____

creaky   _____

attack   _____

plastic   _____

racket   _____

attic   _____

hockey   _____

Lesson 20 Words with the /k/ Sound

Words in Context
Write the missing spelling words.

Be Careful of Rainy Days

Challenge

Circle the other words in the story with the /k/ sound.

One rainy day last week, I decided to

explore the _____. Holding out a lit

_____ in front of me, I crept up the

_____ old stairs. They were barely

covered by a worn-out _____. I kept

looking back over my shoulder as if someone might

sneak up and _____ me from behind.

When I got to the top of the stairs, I looked around and saw all kinds

of _____. In one _____, there was a rusty

metal _____ next to a wicker _____ basket.

Next to these was a trunk filled with sports equipment, including a

_____ stick, ice skates, and a tennis _____.

Nearby, a stuffed _____ seemed to stare at me with one

_____ black eye. Scattered across an old desk were letters,

postcards, and even an old movie _____.

Suddenly, I heard footsteps behind me on the stairs. My mother

appeared and plugged a lamp into a _____. "I'm so glad

you're here to help me clean up this mess," she said with a smile.

Lesson 20 Words with the /k/ Sound

Fun with Words

Write the spelling word that fits each comparison.

1. *Curtain* is to *window* as _____ is to *floor*.

2. *Soccer* is to *grass* as _____ is to *ice*.

3. *Basement* is to *bottom* as _____ is to *top*.

4. *Snake* is to *slither* as _____ is to *hop*.

5. *Bat* is to *baseball* as _____ is to *tennis*.

6. *Straw* is to *basket* as *metal* is to _____.

7. *Bulb* is to *flashlight* as *flame* is to _____.

8. *Curve* is to *circle* as _____ is to *square*.

9. *Hug* is to *friend* as _____ is to *enemy*.

10. *Lunchbox* is to *lunch* as *basket* is to _____.

Words Across the Curriculum

Say each science word. Then, write the word.

1. climate _____   3. volcano _____

2. cricket _____   4. compound _____

Write each science word next to its definition.

1. a substance made of two or more elements _____

2. a hopping insect related to a grasshopper _____

3. a mountain that ejects lava and hot rocks _____

4. the weather patterns in an area _____

Lesson 20 Words with the /k/ Sound

Words in Writing

Describe a place in your home where many things are stored. Use at least four words from the box.

_____

_____

_____

_____

_____

_____

junk	kangaroo	ticket	creaky	racket	climate	volcano
socket	corner	candle	attack	attic	compound	cricket
carpet	picnic	bucket	plastic	hockey		

Dictionary Practice

Write four words from the box that have each sound listed below. You might use a word in more than one column.

Short a Sound	Short i Sound	Short o Sound
_____	_____	_____
_____	_____	_____
_____	_____	_____
_____	_____	_____

Lesson 21 Words with the /s/ Sound

Say each word. Listen for the /s/ sound. Then, write each word.

Spelling Tip	The /s/ sound can be spelled **c** or **s**.

Spelling Words

silent _____

suit _____

special _____

sorry _____

notice _____

ceiling _____

promise _____

sudden _____

cereal _____

select _____

circus _____

office _____

sentence _____

balance _____

celebrate _____

Lesson 21 Words with the /s/ Sound

Words in Context

Write the missing spelling words.

Challenge

Circle the other words in the story with the /s/ sound.

Birthday Surprise

Last Saturday was my birthday. As I was

eating my breakfast of _____ and juice, my dad came

downstairs. He was dressed in a _____ and tie. He looked

like he was ready to go to his _____ and work. He had

forgotten his _____ to spend this _____ day

with me.

My dad was very _____ that he had forgotten. He took

me to the mall and let me _____ some games and CDs.

Then, we went to the _____. We had a great time there. I

especially enjoyed watching the acrobats _____ on the

high wire.

When we got back home, our house was

dark and _____. I didn't

_____ anything unusual. All of a

_____, the lights went on. The

_____ was covered with floating

balloons and a banner with a _____ that said, " Have a

great year!" My friends were all there to _____ my birthday!

Lesson 21 Words with the /s/ Sound

Fun with Words

Solve the puzzle with spelling words.

Across

2. a set of clothes

4. words that express a complete thought

6. a vow or word of honor

7. breakfast food

8. fast and without warning

Down

1. see

3. a place to do paperwork

4. without sound

5. a traveling show

Words Across the Curriculum

Say each science word. Then, write the word.

1. solid _____   3. icicle _____

2. surface _____   4. science _____

Write each science word next to the pair of words it belongs with.

1. outside, top   _____

2. frost, snow   _____

3. math, art   _____

4. gas, liquid   _____

Lesson 21 Words with the /s/ Sound

Words in Writing

Write about a day that was important to you. Use at least four words from the box.

_____

_____

_____

_____

_____

silent	sorry	promise	select	sentence	solid	surface
suit	notice	sudden	circus	balance	icicle	science
special	ceiling	cereal	office	celebrate		

Misspelled Words

Read the description. Circle the five misspelled words. Then, write the words correctly.

Last winter, there was a suddin snowstorm during the night. When I went outside the next morning, I noticed that everything was cilent and covered with snow. The surfase of our pond was frozen solud. My sister and I skated on the pond all day. I was sory when the day ended.

_____ _____ _____

_____ _____

Lesson 22 Words with ex-

Say each word. Look for familiar spelling patterns. Then, write each word.

Spelling Tip	The **ex-** spelling usually comes at the beginnings of words.

Spelling Words

except   _____

example   _____

exciting   _____

exactly   _____

extend   _____

expect   _____

excuse   _____

explain   _____

express   _____

exert   _____

exercise   _____

exhausted   _____

excellent   _____

expensive   _____

extremely   _____

Lesson 22 Words with ex-

Words in Context

Write the missing spelling words.

Why Not Try Tennis?

Playing tennis is an _____

way to _____ while playing a fun sport. The match I recently

played is a perfect _____. I didn't really

_____ the match to _____ any longer than

an hour. However, the match ended up taking _____ two

hours and twenty-two minutes. I had to _____ every extra

bit of energy I had to finish the match, but I still lost. I tried not to

_____ my disappointment about losing. Afterwards, my

opponent and I were both _____. We were moving

_____ slowly when we exited the tennis court.

Some people tell me that they don't play tennis because it's too

_____. I think that they just say this as an

_____ not to play. I _____ to them that once

they have a racket and tennis shoes, they don't have to spend any more

money _____ to buy new tennis balls once in a while. I also

tell them that you don't have to be an expert player to enjoy tennis. It's

an _____ game that everyone should try.

Lesson 22 Words with ex-

Fun with Words

Write the spelling word that fits each sentence and rhymes with the underlined word.

1. The police _____ to question the <u>suspect</u>.

2. Isn't it _____ that they're <u>inviting</u> us to the concert?

3. I'd like to _____ my joy for your <u>success</u>.

4. Please _____ why you continue to <u>complain</u>.

5. That <u>sample</u> is an _____ of sandy soil.

6. My mom didn't <u>refuse</u> to _____ me from school today.

7. This spray seems to be an _____ insect <u>repellant</u>.

8. I had to _____ my strongest effort to stay awake and <u>alert</u>.

Words Across the Curriculum

Say each science word. Then, write the word.

1. examine _____   **3.** exhibit _____

2. explode _____   **4.** experiment _____

Write the science word or words that complete each sentence.

1. A dinosaur _____ is on display at the museum.

2. It's important to _____ the results of an

_____ before drawing a conclusion.

3. Some chemicals _____ when they come in contact with oxygen.

Lesson 22 Words with ex-

Words in Writing

Write a persuasive paragraph about a sport you enjoy. Use at least four words from the box.

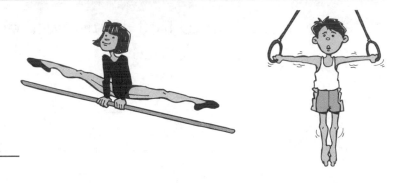

_____

_____

_____

_____

except	exactly	excuse	exert	excellent	examine	explode
example	extend	explain	exercise	expensive	exhibit	experiment
exciting	expect	express	exhausted	extremely		

Dictionary Practice

Write the words from the box in alphabetical order. You will have to look at the third or fourth letter of each word.

1. _____   8. _____   15. _____

2. _____   9. _____   16. _____

3. _____   10. _____   17. _____

4. _____   11. _____   18. _____

5. _____   12. _____   19. _____

6. _____   13. _____

7. _____   14. _____

Review Lessons 19–22

Write the spelling word that rhymes with each word.

1. confess _____

2. mumble _____

3. picket _____

4. boot _____

5. refuse _____

6. peeling _____

7. squeaky _____

8. complain _____

9. handle _____

10. has _____

11. sponge _____

12. jacket _____

13. inviting _____

14. bunk _____

15. pocket _____

Review Lessons 19–22

Write the spelling word that belongs with each pair of words.

16. baseball, soccer, _____

17. word, paragraph, _____

18. model, sample, _____

19. cabin, inn, _____

20. rug, mat, _____

21. basement, garage, _____

22. letter, note, _____

Write the spelling word that is a synonym of each word.

23. pail _____

24. trash _____

25. very _____

26. unsafe _____

27. quiet _____

28. choose _____

29. tired _____

30. operate _____

31. costly _____

Lesson 23 Words with the Prefixes in-, re-, and un-

Say each word. Listen to the first syllable. Then, write each word.

Spelling Tip	The prefix **in-** can mean *not* or *in*. The prefix **re-** often means *again*. The prefix **un-** means *not*.

Spelling Words

remove   _____

unfair   _____

instant   _____

regret   _____

unable   _____

instead   _____

review   _____

unaware   _____

invent   _____

repeat   _____

unless   _____

incorrect   _____

retreat   _____

refuse   _____

incomplete   _____

Lesson 23 Words with the Prefixes in-, re-, and un-

Words in Context

Write the missing spelling words.

Going Fishing

On Saturday morning, my mom

made me _____ my latest math exam. I

had seven _____ answers, and one

problem was _____ because I hadn't

had time to finish it. I had to _____ all of

my calculations. The _____ I finished, my

best friend called and invited me to go fishing with him.

I was _____ that my dad had other plans for me. He

told me to clean my room _____ of going fishing. I thought

it was _____ of him to interrupt my plans, but I couldn't

_____ to clean my room. I was _____ to

_____ any excuses, but I did _____ all those

times when I left my clothes lying on the floor.

I was forced to _____ into my messy bedroom.

_____ I could clean it up quickly, I would have to forget

about fishing. For the next half-hour, I worked incredibly hard to

_____ every piece of trash and dirty clothing from my room.

Finally, I was free to go fishing.

> **Challenge**
>
> Circle the other words in the journal entry with the suffixes **in**-, **re**-, and **un**-.

Lesson 23 Words with the Prefixes **in-**, **re-**, and **un-**

Fun with Words

Write the spelling word that belongs to the same word family as each pair of words.

1. fairness, fairly, _____

2. correction, correctly, _____

3. preview, viewer, _____

4. ability, disabled, _____

5. completely, uncompleted, _____

6. inventor, invention, _____

7. unmoved, removal, _____

8. repetition, repeating, _____

9. refusal, refusing, _____

10. aware, awareness, _____

Words Across the Curriculum

Say each science word. Then, write the word.

1. recycle _____   3. unearth _____

2. instinct _____   4. react _____

Write the science word that completes each sentence.

1. Some metals _____ to oxygen by rusting.

2. Scientists _____ dinosaur bones very carefully.

3. You can _____ glass, paper, and plastic.

4. An _____ is a behavior that an animal is born knowing.

Lesson 23 Words with the Prefixes in-, re-, and un-

Words in Writing

Write a paragraph about something that was difficult for you to learn how to do. Use at least four words from the box.

_____

_____

_____

_____

_____

remove	unable	invent	retreat	unearth
unfair	instead	repeat	refuse	instinct
instant	review	unless	incomplete	react
regret	unaware	incorrect	recycle	

Misspelled Words

Read the paragraph. Circle the five misspelled words. Then, write the words correctly.

I have to admit that I'm completely unabel to play basketball. I tried it once, and it's an experience that I'll never repeet unless I grow about three feet. Insted of getting the ball through the hoop, I could barely throw it over my head. Still, my older brothers wouldn't let me reatreat from the court. I think they had an unfaire advantage because they were much taller than I was.

_____ _____ _____

_____ _____

Lesson 24 Words with the Prefixes **dis-** and **mis-**

Say each word. Listen to the first syllable. Then, write each word.

| **Spelling Tip** | The prefix **dis-** often means *the opposite of*. The prefix **mis-** often means *wrong* or *a lack of*. |

Spelling Words

dislike   _____

mistake   _____

disturb   _____

dismiss   _____

misery   _____

dishonest   _____

disease   _____

misplaced   _____

discuss   _____

disappoint   _____

disagree   _____

misfortune   _____

discover   _____

disappear   _____

distribute   _____

Lesson 24 Words with the Prefixes **dis-** and **mis-**

Words in Context
Write the missing spelling words.

A Surprising Discovery

When I _____ the

newspapers to my customers, I try to

_____ from sight as soon as I

deliver the paper to the last house. I don't want

to _____ the old man who lives

there. I don't _____ him, but some neighbors have told me

that he likes to argue and _____ with everyone.

Today, the old man was sitting on his porch. Much to my dismay, he asked

me to read the paper to him, because he had _____ his reading

glasses. He looked so distressed that I didn't want to _____

him, and I just couldn't make up a _____ excuse. Besides,

maybe he was just lonely. That can be _____ for some people.

I dismounted my bike and sat on the porch while reading the paper

to the old man. Then, he wanted to _____ the news before

he would _____ me from his porch. It didn't take me long to

_____ that I had made a _____ in judging

the old man. He isn't disagreeable at all.

NAME _____

Lesson 24 Words with the Prefixes **dis**- and **mis**-

Fun with Words

Write the spelling word that belongs to the same word family as each word below.

1. placement   _____

2. likely   _____

3. agreement   _____

4. easily   _____

5. fortunately   _____

6. appointment   _____

7. mission   _____

8. covering   _____

Words Across the Curriculum

Say each language arts word. Then, write the word.

1. misprint   _____   3. misspelled _____

2. misquote   _____   4. display   _____

Write the missing language arts words.

A newspaper editor has to make sure that a reporter doesn't

_____ a person who gives information. The editor edits

articles to correct any _____ words and tries to avoid any

kind of _____ in the paper. The editor also chooses photos

to _____ with the articles.

Spectrum Spelling   Lesson 24
Grade 4   Words with the Prefixes **dis**- and **mis**-
110

Lesson 24 Words with the Prefixes **dis**- and **mis**-

Words in Writing

Write directions that tell how you would research and write a newspaper article. Use at least four words from the box.

_____

_____

_____

_____

_____

_____

_____

dislike	misery	discuss	discover	misspelled
mistake	dishonest	disappoint	disappear	misquote
disturb	disease	disagree	distribute	display
dismiss	misplaced	misfortune	misprint	

Dictionary Practice

Write *noun, verb,* or *adjective* to tell what part of speech each word is.

1. discover _____

2. misery _____

3. dishonest _____

4. disease _____

5. disturb _____

6. misfortune _____

7. disagree _____

8. disappear _____

Lesson 25 Words with the Suffix -ly

Say each word. Listen to the last syllable. Then, write each word.

Spelling Tip	Many adverbs end with **ly**.

Spelling Words

lonely _____

wisely _____

barely _____

rapidly _____

finally _____

truly _____

secretly _____

closely _____

eagerly _____

safely _____

totally _____

freely _____

perfectly _____

certainly _____

personally _____

Lesson 25 Words with the Suffix -ly

Words in Context

Write the missing spelling words.

Born Free

Challenge

Circle the other words in the story that end with the suffix **-ly**.

My dad was resting in his hammock so

comfortably that he was _____

awake. A _____ beautiful

butterfly with _____

matched markings on its wings fluttered by

him so _____ that I hardly

saw it. My dad suddenly became alert

and _____ watched the butterfly as it landed on a nearby

flower. I _____ don't know anything about butterflies, but

my dad does. He _____ crept towards it with a net, and I

_____ remained _____ silent.

_____, I hoped that my dad wouldn't catch the butterfly. I

thought it belonged in the garden, moving _____ from

flower to flower. If my dad kept it inside a terrarium, it would

_____ be very _____ all by itself.

_____, my dad had his net just above the butterfly

when our dog suddenly ran over to him and began barking loudly. Just in

time, the butterfly flew _____ away from the net.

Lesson 25 Words with the Suffix -ly

Fun with Words

Unscramble the underlined words to make spelling words. If there is more than one word underlined, combine both words, then unscramble them.

1. A <u>gray</u> <u>eel</u> slithered through the water.   _____

2. The <u>tall</u> boy got a new <u>toy</u> for his birthday.   _____

3. Did you see the gull <u>fly</u> over the <u>sea</u>?   _____

4. The children began to <u>cry</u> when they
   saw the <u>sleet</u> outside.   _____

5. We worked <u>nicely</u> together on our <u>art</u> projects.   _____

6. That <u>lady</u> has a <u>rip</u> in her coat.   _____

7. The soup is made of beef and <u>barley</u>.   _____

8. The farmer <u>nearly</u> slipped when
   he fed the <u>slop</u> to the pigs.   _____

Words Across the Curriculum

Say each social studies word. Then, write the word.

1. recently _____   3. daily   _____

2. monthly _____   4. weekly _____

Write each social studies word next to its meaning.

1. every day   _____

2. not long ago   _____

3. once every seven days   _____

4. once every 28 to 31 days   _____

Lesson 25 Words with the Suffix -ly

Words in Writing
Write a newspaper article that describes
a weather event. Use at least four words
from the box.

_____

_____

_____

_____

_____

lonely	rapidly	secretly	safely	perfectly	recently	monthly
wisely	finally	closely	totally	certainly	daily	weekly
barely	truly	eagerly	freely	personally		

Misspelled Words
Read the article. Circle the five misspelled words. Then, write the words
correctly.

    A sudden storm swept rapidlly though the city today. Some people

egerly reported that they bearly got safely inside their houses before the

storm hit. Others said that they personaly saw a funnel cloud developing.

They wisly took shelter in the basements of their homes.

_____   _____   _____

_____   _____

Lesson 26 Words with the Suffixes -ful and -less

Say each word. Listen to the last syllable. Then, write each word.

Spelling Tip	The suffix -ful means *full of*. The suffix -less means *without*.

Spelling Words

cheerful   _____

colorful   _____

spotless   _____

thankful   _____

graceful   _____

harmless   _____

hopeful   _____

restless   _____

wonderful   _____

frightful   _____

breathless   _____

thoughtful   _____

faithful   _____

motionless   _____

beautiful   _____

Lesson 26 Words with the Suffixes -ful and -less

Words in Context
Write the missing spelling words.

Thanks for the Memories

> **Challenge**
> Circle the other words with the suffix **-ful** or **-less**.

Dear Ms. Johnson,

I'm very _____ to you for the _____ time I had at your camp. I didn't see any _____ spiders; the cabin was so clean that it was truly _____. The _____ blend of blues and yellows inside the cabin always made me feel _____. Also, the view of the peaceful meadow was _____.

Whenever I got _____ from being inside the cabin, I found many things to do outside. I enjoyed observing the _____ deer running through the woods. Although I was _____ with excitement to be so close to them, I was careful to remain _____ so they would know that I was _____.

I also want to let you know how grateful I am to your camp workers for being so helpful and _____. I am _____ that I will be able to return to your camp next year. I will always be a _____ customer.

Sincerely,
Frankie Martinez

Lesson 26 Words with the Suffixes -ful and -less

Fun with Words

Write the spelling word that fits each description.

1. A runner after a race   _____

2. A rainbow in the sky   _____

3. A scary costume   _____

4. A person making a wish   _____

5. A room that's just been cleaned   _____

6. A bike that no one is riding   _____

7. A happy person   _____

8. A bee that doesn't sting   _____

9. A dog that loves its owner   _____

10. A student writing a report   _____

Words Across the Curriculum

Say each social studies word. Then, write the word.

1. careless _____   3. worthless _____

2. eventful _____   4. respectful _____

Write the social studies word next to its meaning.

1. without value   _____

2. full of courtesy   _____

3. full of things to see and do   _____

4. without caution or attention   _____

Lesson 26 Words with the Suffixes -**ful** and -**less**

Words in Writing

Write a letter thanking someone for something they did for you. Use at least four words from the box.

_____

_____

_____

_____

_____

_____

_____

cheerful	graceful	wonderful	faithful	worthless
colorful	harmless	frightful	motionless	eventful
spotless	hopeful	breathless	beautiful	respectful
thankful	restless	thoughtful	careless	

Dictionary Practice

Write the root word of each spelling word below.

1. colorful _____

2. graceful _____

3. breathless _____

4. thoughtful _____

5. wonderful _____

6. harmless _____

7. thankful _____

8. beautiful _____

Review Lessons 23–26

Write the spelling word that is an antonym of each word.

1. ungrateful   _____

2. dangerous   _____

3. happiness   _____

4. truthful   _____

5. slowly   _____

6. openly   _____

7. ugly   _____

8. clumsy   _____

9. foolishly   _____

10. alert   _____

Write the spelling word that completes each sentence.

11. I can't leave _____ I ask my dad.

12. My brother looks _____ in his skeleton costume.

13. The frog hopped away the _____ I let go of it.

14. Sydney _____ her book and searched the whole house for it.

15. We have to _____ our muddy shoes before we go inside.

Review Lessons 23–26

Write the spelling word that is a synonym of each word.

16. wrong _____

17. illness _____

18. surely _____

19. completely _____

20. loyal _____

21. create _____

22. unmoving _____

23. find _____

24. error _____

25. unluckiness _____

26. honestly _____

27. happy _____

28. redo _____

29. lastly _____

30. bother _____

Lesson 27 Number Words

Say each word. Look for familiar spelling patterns. Then, write each word.

Spelling Tip	Many number words have familiar spelling patterns.

Spelling Words

thirty _____

sixteen _____

eleven _____

billion _____

forty _____

thirteen _____

fifteen _____

eighteen _____

fifty _____

fourteen _____

million _____

nineteen _____

twenty _____

seventeen _____

twelve _____

Lesson 27 Number Words

Words in Writing

Write the missing spelling words.

Numbers

Numbers can be added and described

in all kinds of ways. For example, _____ eggs or doughnuts

make a dozen. Two quarters equal _____ cents, three dimes

equal _____ cents, and three nickels equal

_____ cents. Two

weeks include _____

days, and two baseball teams have

_____ players on the

field at one time.

Two spiders together have _____ legs. Ten squares

have _____ angles, while three triangles plus two squares

have _____ angles. One less than a dozen is

_____, and one more is _____. Two times ten

is _____, and one less than that is _____.

Very large numbers describe some other things. Coal and oil formed

more than a _____ years ago. There are more than a

_____ stars in our galaxy.

Lesson 27 Number Words

Fun with Words

Solve each math problem with a numeral that represents a spelling word.
Then, write the spelling word.

1. $10 + 7 = $ _____   _____

2. $100 - 50 = $ _____   _____

3. $32 \div 2 = $ _____   _____

4. $6 \times 5 = $ _____   _____

5. $77 \div 7 = $ _____   _____

6. $5 \times 8 = $ _____   _____

7. $40 - 28 = $ _____   _____

8. $90 \div 6 = $ _____   _____

9. $39 \div 3 = $ _____   _____

10. $10 \times 2 = $ _____   _____

Words Across the Curriculum

Say each math word. Then, write the word.

1. numeral _____   3. decimal _____

2. product _____   4. fraction _____

Write the word or words that complete each sentence.

1. A _____ is a part of a whole that can also be

   represented as a _____ .

2. Any number can be spelled out or written as a _____ .

3. A _____ results from multiplying two or more numbers.

Lesson 27 Number Words

Words in Writing

Write a paragraph describing what you might be doing at different ages in your life. Use at least four words from the box.

_____

_____

_____

_____

_____

thirty	billion	fifteen	fourteen	twenty	numeral	product
sixteen	forty	eighteen	million	seventeen	decimal	fraction
eleven	thirteen	fifty	nineteen	twelve		

Misspelled Words

Read the paragraph. Circle the five misspelled words. Then, write the words correctly.

Right now, I'm elevin years old. When I turn forteen, I'll be a teenager. I will be glad to get my diver's license when I'm sixteen. When I'm eigtteen, I'll be able to vote. Maybe I'll make a millon dollars by the time I'm thirtey.

_____   _____   _____

_____   _____

Lesson 28 Words That End with -**tion**, -**ture**, and -**ure**

Say each word. Listen to the last syllable. Then, write each word.

Spelling Tip	The /shən/ sound is often spelled **tion**. The /chər/ sound is often spelled **ture**. The /yər/ sound is often spelled **ure**.

Spelling Words

nation   _____

moisture   _____

direction   _____

figure   _____

mention   _____

creature   _____

vacation   _____

pleasure   _____

condition   _____

location   _____

feature   _____

attention   _____

adventure   _____

protection   _____

furniture   _____

Lesson 28 Words That End with -tion, -ture, and -ure

Words in Context
Write the missing spelling words.

Dream House

Are you looking for the perfect

_____ home for you and your family? We have a house for

sale in a wonderful _____ on the beach. The house is the

creation of a famous builder. It's in excellent _____, and some

of the _____ and pictures inside will be sold with the house.

There's a huge deck that faces in the _____ of the ocean.

It's a real _____ to sit so close to the shore that you can feel

the _____ from the waves on your skin.

Another great _____ of the house is that it's next to one

of the most secluded nature preserves in the _____. You're

sure to have an interesting _____ every time you visit it. It's

common for an unusual _____ moving in the preserve to

catch the _____ of a person walking near it. The motion is

often caused by an unusual _____ that is under the

_____ of the government.

Please call us and _____ this ad. Hurry! This treasure will

be gone in the very near future.

Lesson 28 Words That End with -tion, -ture, and -ure

Fun with Words

Write the spelling word or words that fit each sentence and have the same ending as the underlined word.

1. Please turn your _____ to the _____ of the <u>motion</u> picture on the screen.

2. It's always great to have an _____ surrounded by <u>nature</u>.

3. Did you <u>mention</u> the _____ of your favorite place to take a _____?

4. I hope there won't be any _____ on the patio _____ in the <u>future</u>.

5. The shadowy form of a mysterious _____ appeared in the <u>pasture</u>.

Words Across the Curriculum

Say each science word. Then, write the word.

1. caution _____   3. solution _____

2. measure _____   4. temperature _____

Write the science word or words that complete each sentence.

1. Ocean water is a common _____ made of salt and water.

2. You can _____ the _____ of an object in degrees Fahrenheit or Celsius.

3. Always use _____ when working with chemicals.

Lesson 28 Words That End with **-tion**, **-ture**, and **-ure**

Words in Writing

Write an ad that you could use to convince people to buy something that you own. Use at least four words from the box.

_____

_____

_____

_____

_____

_____

nation	mention	condition	adventure	solution
moisture	creature	location	protection	measure
direction	vacation	feature	furniture	temperature
figure	pleasure	attention	caution	

Dictionary Practice

Write the root word of each word below. Use a dictionary if you need help.

1. location _____

2. moisture _____

3. direction _____

4. pleasure _____

5. protection _____

6. vacation _____

7. attention _____

8. adventure _____

Lesson 29 Adjectives That End with -**er** and -**est**

Say each word. Listen to the second syllable and the third syllable, if there is one. Then, write each word.

Spelling Tip	For adjectives that end with **y**, change the **y** to **i** before adding **er** or **est**.

Spelling Words

happy   _____

cloudy   _____

uglier   _____

heaviest   _____

pretty   _____

happier   _____

cloudiest   _____

ugly   _____

heavier   _____

happiest   _____

prettier   _____

ugliest   _____

heavy   _____

cloudier   _____

prettiest   _____

Lesson 29 Adjectives That End with -er and -est

Words in Context
Write the missing spelling words.

An Unkind Princess

There once was a princess who was never

_____ than when she was playing with her golden balls. One

_____ day, the princess took three balls that she thought

were _____ than the others into the garden. Although they

were _____, the princess liked to toss them into the air. The

princess thought they were the _____ sight she had ever seen.

As she played, the _____ of the balls rolled into a deep well.

The princess was not _____ about this, and she began to cry.

Soon, an _____ frog poked his head out of the water.

"I'll get the ball if I can eat lunch with you at your dining table," said

the frog. Then, I'll be the _____ creature in the world instead

of the _____."

The princess's face became _____ than the sky as she

imagined the frog at her father's fine table. The frog seemed

_____ to her than ever. Still, the sky was the

_____ that she had ever seen. The princess couldn't go

inside without her _____ golden ball. Her heart felt

_____ every minute.

Lesson 29 Adjectives That End with -er and -est

Fun with Words

Unscramble the underlined words to make spelling words. If there is more than one word underlined, combine both words, then unscramble them.

1. As I began to eat my <u>rice</u>, I heard a <u>loud</u> noise. _____

2. Be careful not to <u>trip</u> on the rocks under the <u>tree</u>. _____

3. Let's <u>eat</u> the honey from the bee's <u>hives</u>. _____

4. I made a small <u>ship</u> out of paper and <u>tape</u>. _____

5. When my <u>pet</u> mouse gets tired,
   <u>it</u> likes to <u>rest</u> on my lap. _____

6. Mother took the pie <u>out</u> of the oven
   and <u>sliced</u> it into pieces. _____

Words Across the Curriculum

Say each science word. Then, write the word.

1. sunnier _____

2. sunniest _____

3. healthier _____

4. healthiest _____

Write the missing science words.

The _____ plants get just the right amount of sunlight

and water. Some plants need to be grown in _____

locations than other plants. A plant that needs constant light might need

to be moved to the _____ spot you can find. The plant will

soon become _____.

Lesson 29 Adjectives That End with -er and -est

Words in Writing

Write an ending to the story about the princess
and the frog. Use at least four words from the box.

_____

_____

_____

_____

_____

happy	heaviest	cloudiest	happiest	heavy	sunnier	sunniest
cloudy	pretty	ugly	prettier	cloudier	healthier	healthiest
uglier	happier	heavier	ugliest	prettiest		

Misspelled Words

Read the ending to the story. Circle the four misspelled words. Then, write
the words correctly.

   The king was not happi with his daughter for trying to break her promise
to the frog. He told her that her actions were much ugleir than the way the
poor frog looked to her. He ordered the princess to find the frog as soon as
the cloudy sky became sunnyier. The princess was sorry that she had been
so cruel to the frog. When she found him, she felt much happyier.

_____   _____

_____   _____

NAME _____

Lesson 30 More Easily Misspelled Words

Say each word. Look for familiar and unfamiliar spelling patterns. Then, write the word.

Spelling Tip	Some words have unusual spellings. You have to remember how these words are spelled.

Spelling Words

believe _____

guess _____

century _____

machine _____

library _____

probably _____

recognize _____

separate _____

question _____

portrait _____

citizen _____

enough _____

government _____

biography _____

especially _____

Lesson 30 More Easily Misspelled Words

Words in Context

Write the missing spelling words.

Time for Research

For social studies class, I had to read

a _____ about a person

whose work I _____ was

_____ important to my

daily life. I didn't have

_____ information at home,

so I went to the _____ to do some research. I wanted a

quiet place to work, so I found a desk that was _____ from

the main research area.

I wasn't sure whether I wanted to read about a person who invented

an important _____ or a person who helped form the

_____ of our country. I was gazing around the room when I

saw a _____ of a person I didn't _____. My

_____ was that it was _____ a famous

_____ from the eighteenth _____. My

_____ was soon answered. The plaque under the painting

identified the person as the founder of the city.

Lesson 30 More Easily Misspelled Words

Fun with Words

Write the spelling word that completes each analogy.

1. <u>Command</u> is to <u>order</u> as _____ is to <u>ask</u>.

2. <u>Member</u> is to <u>club</u> as _____ is to <u>country</u>.

3. <u>Theater</u> is to <u>movie</u> as _____ is to <u>book</u>.

4. <u>Statue</u> is to <u>sculpture</u> as _____ is to <u>painting</u>.

5. <u>Combine</u> is to <u>unite</u> as _____ is to <u>divide</u>.

6. <u>Hammer</u> is to <u>tool</u> as <u>car</u> is to _____.

7. <u>Fact</u> is to <u>know</u> as <u>faith</u> is to _____.

8. <u>Ten</u> is to <u>decade</u> as one <u>hundred</u> is to _____.

9. <u>Surely</u> is to <u>certainly</u> as <u>possibly</u> is to _____.

Words Across the Curriculum

Say each science word. Then, write the word.

1. weather _____

2. equator _____

3. dinosaur _____

4. stomach_____

Write the missing science words.

1. The _____ separates the northern and southern hemispheres.

2. A _____ skeleton contains hundreds of bones.

3. Different climates on Earth experience different types of _____.

4. A female kangaroo has a pouch on her _____ for carrying babies.

Lesson 30 More Easily Misspelled Words

Words in Writing

Write a paragraph about an
important American citizen. Use
at least four words from the box.

_____

_____

_____

_____

believe	machine	recognize	portrait	biography	weather	equator
guess	library	separate	citizen	especially	dinosaur	stomach
century	probably	question	enough	government		

Dictionary Practice

Write the spelling words that fit in each column below. Some words belong
in more than one column.

/e/ Sound	Long e Sound	Long i Sound
_____	_____	_____
_____	_____	_____
_____	_____	_____
_____	_____	_____
_____	_____	
	_____	
	_____	

Lesson 31 Compound Words

Say each word. Look for the two smaller words in each compound word. Then, write the word.

Spelling Tip	Many compound words are made of smaller words with familiar spelling patterns.

Spelling Words

highway   _____

football   _____

classmate   _____

skateboard   _____

motorcycle   _____

newspaper   _____

background   _____

notebook   _____

stoplight   _____

sideline   _____

crosswalk   _____

somewhere   _____

grandstand   _____

brainstorm   _____

scrapbook   _____

Lesson 31 Compound Words

Words in Context

Write the missing spelling words.

At the Park

Challenge

Circle the other compound words in the journal entry.

Sometimes, I walk to the park near my home in the afternoon. I turn left at the second _____ and then follow the _____ into the park. Usually, I walk by myself along the _____ of the _____ field and find an empty bench _____ near the woods. I like to blend into the _____ of the park and watch other people.

Today, I saw a college student sitting under a tree and reading a _____. There were a few old ladies on another bench looking at a _____ filled with photographs of themselves from their childhood. A _____ of mine from school whizzed past them on a _____.

The bleachers of the _____ were deserted. The sunlit park was quiet except for the sudden roar of a _____ speeding down the _____ near the park. I decided to take out a pen and a _____ from my backpack. This seemed like a good time to _____ ideas for a story I have to write.

Lesson 31 Compound Words

Fun with Words

Write the spelling word that completes each sign and includes one word from the underlined compound word.

1. Please don't <u>jaywalk</u>! Use the _____ instead.

2. We need to paint the <u>outline</u> of the field to make each end

_____.

3. Buy tickets to the fair at the <u>newsstand</u> next to the _____.

4. Come and enjoy the scenic _____ of our <u>campground</u>.

5. Shop here for a new bicycle, <u>surfboard</u>, or _____!

6. Buy one ticket and your <u>teammate</u> or _____ gets one.

7. Make sure you bring your <u>textbook</u> and a _____ to class.

8. The <u>football</u> field and the _____ court are closed.

Words Across the Curriculum

Say each science word. Then, write the word.

1. earthquake _____   **3.** waterfall _____

2. rattlesnake _____   **4.** heartbeat _____

Write the missing science words.

1. A _____ make a warning sound with its tail.

2. During exercise, a person's _____ becomes faster.

3. A severe _____ can destroy buildings, roads, and bridges.

4. A _____ forms when a stream rushes over rocks that resist erosion.

Lesson 31 Compound Words

Words in Writing

Write a description of a hobby that you enjoy. Use at least four words from the box.

_____

_____

_____

_____

_____

highway	motorcycle	stoplight	grandstand	waterfall
football	newspaper	sideline	brainstorm	rattlesnake
classmate	background	crosswalk	scrapbook	heartbeat
skateboard	notebook	somewhere	earthquake	

Misspelled Words

Read the description. Circle the five misspelled words. Then, write the words correctly.

    I like to collect photos and newpaper clippings for my scrapebook. I include articles about my brother's football team. I have a photo of my dad riding his motercycle on the hiway. I also have a photo of myself on the skatboard I got for my birthday.

_____   _____   _____

_____   _____

Review Lessons 27-31

Write the spelling word that names each number.

1. 19   _____

2. 40   _____

3. 11   _____

4. 13   _____

5. 20   _____

6. 15   _____

7. 1,000,000   _____

8. 30   _____

Write the spelling word that is an antonym of each word or phrase.

9. most beautiful   _____

10. combined   _____

11. lighter   _____

12. pain   _____

13. sad   _____

14. dryness   _____

15. answer   _____

16. no place   _____

17. sunniest   _____

18. most sorrowful   _____

Review Lessons 27-31

Write the spelling word that fits with each group of words.

19. hockey, soccer, _____

20. million, trillion, _____

21. rugs, curtains, _____

22. republic, country, _____

23. shape, outline, _____

24. bicycle, scooter, _____

25. year, decade, _____

26. street, road, _____

27. safety, preservation, _____

28. trait, characteristic, _____

Write the spelling word that is a synonym of each word.

29. ideas _____

30. setting _____

31. beast _____

32. dozen _____

33. stadium _____

34. place _____

A

B

ac·tors *pl. n.* People who act in plays, movies, television shows, and other media, usually in fictional roles.

ad·dress *n.* The location to which mail or goods can be sent to a person. *v.* To speak to.

ad·ven·ture *n.* An exciting, dangerous, or unusual experience.

af·ford *v.* To have enough money to spare; to be able to provide.

a·gainst *prep.* In contact with; not in favor of or in combat with.

a·gent *n.* A person who acts as the representative of another.

a·lign *v.* To adjust or bring into line.

al·though *conj.* Even though; despite the fact that.

a·maze *v.* To overwhelm with surprise or wonder.

an·gle *n.* A shape made by two straight lines meeting at a point.

an·kle *n.* The joint that connects the foot with the leg.

an·swer *n.* A written or spoken reply, as to a question; a result or solution, as to a problem. *v.* To respond.

art·ists' *pl. poss.* Belonging to people who practice the fine arts of painting, sculpture, architecture, literature, music, dance, or theater.

at·tack *v.* To apply force or to assault; to work on energetically. *n.* A sudden action of aggression; assault.

at·ten·tion *n.* Observation, notice, or mental concentration.

a·while *adv.* For a short time.

ba·bies' *poss. pl.* Belonging to infants or very young children.

back·ground *n.* The area or surface behind which objects are represented.

ba·con *n.* Meat from the side and back of a pig.

badge *n.* A symbol worn for identification.

bal·ance *n.* The state of a body or object having a steady position; a tool for determining the weight of something. *v.* To keep in a steady state or position.

ban·ner *n.* A piece of cloth with a symbol or message on it, such as a flag.

bare·ly *adv.* Scarcely; hardly.

bas·ket *n.* A container made of woven material.

beast *n.* Any animal other than a human, especially a large, four-legged animal.

beau·ti·ful *adj.* Being pleasing to the eye.

beet *n.* The root from a cultivated plant that can be used as a vegetable.

be·fore *adv.* Earlier; previously. *prep.* In front of.

be·have *v.* To act or function in a certain manner.

be·lieve *v.* To accept as true or real.

be·low *adv.* In or to a lower place. *prep.* Lower in rank, degree, or position.

bi·cy·cle *n.* A two-wheeled vehicle propelled by pedals.

bil·lion *n.* A thousand million.

bi·og·ra·phy *n.* A researched and accurate report of the life and accomplishments of a person written by another person.

bi·ome *n.* A major type of habitat, such as a jungle or grasslands.

blan·ket *n.* A covering used on a bed for warmth; something that evenly covers a surface.

bor·der *n.* A political or geographic boundary; a decorative or protective margin or edge.

bot·tom *n.* The lowest or deepest part of anything.

brain *n.* The main organ of the body's nervous system, responsible for control of the body, the senses, and coordination; the center of thought and emotion.

brain·storm *n.* A sudden idea or inspiration. *v.* To think and contribute ideas without boundaries.

brave *adj.* Having courage; willing to face danger or pain.

breathe *v.* To draw air into and expel from the lungs.

breath·less *adj.* Without breath.

bridge *n.* A structure allowing passage over two bodies of land divided by water or some other gap.

broke *v.* Past tense of *break*. Cracked or split into pieces; caused to end.

broth·ers' *pl. poss.* Belonging to males who share the same parents as another person.

bub·ble *n.* A small body of gas contained inside a liquid.

buck·et *n.* A vessel used to carry liquids or solids; a pail.

built *v.* Past tense of build. Created or fashioned.

bunch *n.* A cluster or group of like items.

C

cab·bage *n.* A vegetable similar in shape to lettuce.

ca·bin *n.* A shelter in the woods, usually made of logs.

ca·ble *adj.* Sent through wires or a satellite. *n.* A heavy rope made from fiber or steel.

cac·tus *n.* A plant that lives primarily in desert regions.

cal·ves *pl. n.* Young offspring of cows.

cam·er·a *n.* A device for taking photographs.

can·dle *n.* A wax form with a wick used for light.

ca·pac·i·ty *n.* The maximum amount of matter, especially liquid, that a container can hold.

car·bon *n.* A nonmetallic element that is present in all living and once-living material.

care·less *adj.* Without care or concern.

car·pet *n.* A thick, woven floor covering.

cau·tion *n.* Care regarding danger or risk; a warning advising careful planning or procedure.

ceil·ing *n.* The overhead covering of a room.

cel·e·brate *v.* To observe with ceremonies, rejoicing, or festivity.

cel·er·y *n.* A green vegetable with an edible stalk.

cen·tral *adj.* In, near, or at the center.

ce·re·al *n.* An edible grain eaten as a breakfast food.

cer·tain *adj.* Very sure; without any doubt.

cer·tain·ly *adv.* Definitely.

chance *n.* The possibility of something happening; opportunity.

chap·ter *n.* A major division of a book.

charge *v.* To ask a price for something. *n.* The required price; the amount of electrical energy that an object has.

cheap *adj.* Inexpensive; low in cost; of poor quality.

cheer·ful *adj.* Having or being in good spirits.

cheese *n.* A food made from milk.

cher·ry *n.* A small, round, deep red or purplish red fruit with a small, hard stone.

chief *n.* The person of highest rank *adj.* Most important.

child·ren's *pl. poss.* Belonging to young people.

choke *v.* To prevent or interrupt the breathing.

chore *n.* A daily task.

cir·cus *n.* A traveling show featuring clowns, acrobats, trained animals, and other acts.

cit·i·zen *n.* A resident of a town, city, or country.

class·mate *n.* A member of one's class.

cli·mate *n.* The weather conditions of a certain region.

close *v.* To shut.

close·ly *adv.* Being near in time, space, or relationship.

clos·et *n.* A small cabinet, compartment, or room for storage.

clothes *n.* Articles made from cloth and worn on the body.

cloud·i·er *adj.* having more clouds than another.

cloud·i·est *adj.* Having the most clouds of all.

cloud·y *adj.* Having clouds.

color·ful *adj.* Having many colors.

col·umn *n.* A vertical list of numbers; a pillar used in constructing buildings.

comb *n.* A toothed device used for smoothing and arranging hair.

com·pound *n.* A mixture made of two or more parts or substances.

con·di·tion *n.* The state of existence of a person or object.

con·tin·ue *v.* To maintain without interruption a course or condition.

cor·ner *n.* The point formed when two surfaces or lines meet and form an angle.

cot·ton *n.* A plant grown for its soft, fluffy fibers, which are used to make cloth; the fabric made from the fibers of such a plant.

course *n.* The act of moving in a path from one point to another.

court *n.* A place where justice is carried out and trials are held; an area marked off for playing a sport.

crea·ture *n.* Any living being, especially a member of the animal kingdom.

crick·et *n.* A leaping insect.

croak *n.* A hoarse, raspy cry such as that made by a frog.

cross·walk *n.* A marked area of a street, usually at an intersection, for people to cross.

cur·rent *n.* a stream within a body of water or air that constantly flows in the same path. *adj.* Belonging or occurring in the present time.

curve *n.* A line that has a smooth slope.

cus·tom *n.* An accepted practice of a community or people.

cus·to·mers' *poss. pl.* Belonging to people who buy items from sellers.

cy·cle *n.* A series of events that occur repeatedly.

cyl·in·der *n.* A long, round object that is either hollow or solid.

D

dai·ly *adj.* Happening every day.

danc·ers' *poss. pl.* Belonging to people who move their bodies to music.

dan·ger *n.* Something unsafe, causing injury or loss.

dan·ger·ous *adj.* Having danger.

de·cide *v.* To settle; to make up one's mind.

dec·i·mal *n.* A proper fraction based on the number 10 and indicated by the use of a decimal point.

de·gree *n.* A unit of cold or heat on a thermometer.

des·ert *n.* A hot, dry, barren region of land that receives very little rainfall.

de·sign *n.* A plan or sketch made to serve as a guide; a pattern. *v.* To invent or create in the mind; to draw and sketch an idea or outline.

dif·fer·ent *adj.* Not the same.

di·no·saur *n.* Any extinct reptile from prehistoric times.

di·rec·tion *n.* An instruction, order or command; the path or line along which something points.

dis·a·gree *v.* To vary in opinion; to differ; to argue.

dis·ap·pear *v.* To vanish; to drop from sight.

dis·ap·point *v.* To fail to satisfy; to let down.

dis·a·ppoint·ed *adj.* Unhappy because something one hoped for has failed.

dis·cov·er *v.* To make known or visible; to find for the first time.

dis·cuss *v.* To hold a conversation; to talk.

dis·ease *n.* A sickness, often spread from one person to another.

dis·hon·est *adj.* Lacking honesty; coming from falseness.

dis·like *v.* To have no appreciation or respect for something.

dis·miss *v.* To allow to leave; to remove from a position.

dis·play *n.* An exhibit. *v.* To show or put on exhibit.

dis·tance *n.* Separation in time or space.

dis·trib·ute *v.* To divide among many.

dis·turb *v.* To destroy the balance or rest of someone or something.

ditch *n.* A trench in the ground.

di·vide *v.* To separate into halves or portions and give out in shares.

dou·ble *adj.* Twice as much.

drive *v.* To operate a vehicle.

du·ty *n.* Something a person must or ought to do; an obligation or responsibility.

E

ea·ger·ly *adv.* With desire.

ear·ly *adj.* Occurring near the beginning of a period of time; before the expected time.

Earth *n.* The third planet from the sun.

earth·quake *n.* A sudden movement of Earth's crust that causes violent shaking on the surface of Earth.

ef·fort *n.* An attempt; a use of physical or mental energy to do something.

eigh·teen *n.* The number after seventeen and before nineteen.

eighth *n.* Number eight in a series.

e·lec·tric *adj.* Relating to energy, especially energy carried by protons and electrons through wires.

el·e·ment *n.* A substance that contains only one type of atoms.

e·lev·en *n.* The number after ten and before twelve.

en·er·gy *n.* The ability or power to move or work.

English *n.* A language spoken and written in the United States, England, and other parts of the world.

e·nough *adj.* Adequate to satisfy demands or needs.

e·qua·tor *n.* The imaginary circle around Earth that separates the northern and southern hemispheres.

es·cape *v.* To break free from capture or restraint.

es·pe·cial·ly *adv.* Gaining or deserving special consideration.

e·vent·ful *adv.* Full of happenings.

eve·ry·one *pron.* All persons.

ex·act·ly *adv.* Accurately or precisely; perfectly.

ex·am·ine *v.* To observe or inspect.

ex·am·ple *n.* A representative as a sample.

ex·cel·lent *adj.* Of the best quality.

ex·cept *prep.* But; with the omission or exclusion of.

ex·cit·ing *adj.* Fun-filled; entertaining.

ex·cuse *n.* A reason given to explain something.

ex·er·cise *n.* A physical workout; a drill or repeated activity to gain skill.

ex·ert *v.* To make a strenuous effort.

ex·haust·ed *adj.* Extremely tired.

ex·hib·it *n.* A display. *v.* To display, or put up for public view.

ex·it *n.* A way or passage out.

ex·pect *v.* To look forward to something as probable or certain.

ex·pen·sive *adj.* Costing a lot of money; high-priced.

ex·per·i·ment *n.* An act or test performed to demonstrate or illustrate a truth.

ex·pert *n.* A person having great knowledge, experience, or skill in a certain field.

ex·plain *v.* To make understandable; to make clear.

ex·plode *v.* To burst or blow up violently with a loud noise.

ex·plore *v.* To examine and investigate in a systematic way.

ex·port *v.* To carry or send goods or raw materials to other countries for resale or trade.

ex·press *v.* To put into words; to show outwardly through words, actions, or art.

ex·tend *v.* To stretch or open to full length.

ex·tra *adj.* Over and above what is normal, required, or expected.

ex·treme·ly *adv.* To a great or excessive degree.

F

faith·ful *adj.* True and trustworthy in the performance of duty, promises, or obligations.

fam·i·lies' *poss. pl.* belonging to groups of parents and their children.

fea·ture *n.* An important part or characteristic of something; a part of the face.

fetch *v.* To go after and return with.

field *n.* A piece of land with few or no trees; an area of land cleared and set aside for the playing of a sport.

fif·teen *n.* The number after fourteen and before sixteen.

fif·ty *n.* The number after forty-nine and before fifty-one.

fight *n.* A struggle or argument. *v.* To struggle against in combat; to quarrel; to argue.

fig·ure *n.* The visible form of something; the human form or body.

fin·al·ly *adv.* At last; after a long time.

fin·ish *v.* To bring to or reach an end.

fla·vor *n.* A distinctive taste of something.

flute *n.* A high-pitched musical woodwind instrument.

foot·ball *n.* A team game whose object is to get the ball over a goal line or between goalposts by running, passing or kicking; the ball used in such a game.

force *n.* Energy or power; strength; *v.* To compel or make happen by force.

for·ty *n.* The number after thirty-nine and after forty-one.

fort *n.* A building used as protection against an army.

four·teen *n.* The number after thirteen and before fifteen.

fowl *n.* A bird used as food or hunted as game.

frac·tion *n.* A small part; in mathematics, an indicated quantity less than a whole number.

free·ly *adv.* Without being held back or restrained; with an easy manner.

friends' *poss. pl.* Belonging to people personally well-known and liked.

fright·ful *adj.* Causing fear; disgusting or shocking.

fur·ni·ture *n.* Movable articles, such as chairs and tables, used in a home, office, or other interior.

fur·ther *adj.* Beyond; more distant in time or space.

G

gar·bage *n.* Trash or waste material.

gath·er *v.* To bring or come together into one place or group.

gen·tle *adj.* Not harsh, severe, rough, or loud.

geese *pl. n.* More than one goose.

germ *n.* A tiny living organism, especially one that causes disease.

gov·ern·ment *n.* An organization that rules or directs a country, state, or city.

grace·ful *adj.* Full of seemingly effortless beauty and charm of movement.

grand·moth·ers' *pl. poss. n.* Belonging to the mothers of people's fathers or mothers.

grand·stand *n.* A seating area for people to view an outdoor event.

graph *n.* A diagram that represents the relationship between sets of things.

great *adj.* Very large in size or volume.

groan *n.* A long, deep sound of pain or disapproval. *v.* To utter a deep, prolonged sound of pain or disapproval.

grown *adj.* Having matured or increased in size.

guess *n.* An opinion formed without complete knowledge. *v.* To make a judgment or form an opinion on uncertain or incomplete knowledge.

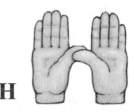

H

halves *n.* Two equal parts of a whole.

ham·ster's *poss. n.* Belonging to a large rodent with large cheek pouches and a short tail.

hap·pen *v.* To occur or come to pass.

hap·pi·er *adj.* More happy than another.

hap·pi·est *adj.* Most happy of all.

hap·py *adj.* Enjoying contentment and well-being.

harm·less *adj.* Unable to cause pain.

health·i·er *adj.* In a better state or having better health than another.

health·i·est *adj.* In the best state or having the best health of all.

healthy *adj.* Being in good physical condition.

heart·beat *n.* A pulsation of the heart.

heav·i·er *adj.* Weighing more than another.

heav·i·est *adj.* Weighing more than all others.

heav·y *adj.* Of great weight.

heel *n.* The rounded back part of the human foot under and behind the ankle.

height *n.* The distance from the bottom to the top of something.

high·way *n.* A main road connecting towns and cities.

his·to·ry *n.* Past events, especially those involving human affairs.

hitch *v.* To fasten or tie temporarily with a knot.

hock·ey *n.* A game played on ice between two teams of skaters.

hol·low *adj.* Having a cavity or empty space inside.

hon·ey *n.* A sweet, sticky substance made by bees from the nectar gathered from flowers.

hope·ful *adj.* Having belief that something can happen.

hunch *v.* To bend or stoop.

hur·ry *v.* To move or cause to move with haste.

hy·dro·gen *n.* A colorless, normally odorless, highly flammable gas.

I

i·ci·cle *n.* A hanging spike of ice formed by dripping water that freezes.

im·age *n.* A representation of the form and features of someone or something.

in·clude *v.* To have as a part or member.

in·com·plete *adj.* Not finished.

in·cor·rect *adj.* Wrong; not correct.

in·spect *v.* To examine or look at very carefully for flaws.

in·stant *n.* A very short time; a moment.

in·stead *adv.* Rather than something else.

in·stinct *n.* A tendency for an animal to act in a certain way that is inherited, not learned.

in·ter·sect *v.* To divide by cutting through or across.

in·vent *v.* To create by an original effort or design.

in·vite *v.* To request the presence or participation of a person.

is·land *n.* A piece of land smaller than a continent and completely surrounded by water.

is·sue *n.* A subject that is under discussion or consideration.

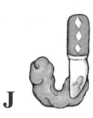

J

jazz *n.* A kind of music that has a strong rhythmic structure.

jew·el *n.* A precious stone.

jock·ey *n.* A person who rides a horse in races as a profession.

jum·ble *n.* A confused or disordered mixture. *v.* To mix in a confused mass.

junk *n.* Discarded or unused items.

ju·ry *n.* A group of people summoned to serve at a court trial to give a verdict according to evidence presented.

jus·tice *n.* The principle of moral or ideal rightness.

K

kan·ga·roo *n.* A jumping marsupial of Australia, with short forelegs, large hind limbs, and a large tail.

ket·tle *n.* A large, metal pot for stewing or boiling.

kni·ves *pl. n.* Tools used to cut items.

L

land·form *n.* A feature of land, such as a mountain or cliff.

la·sa·gna *n.* Pasta in the shape of long strips.

least *adj.* The smallest amount.

leaves *pl. n.* More than one leaf.

lem·on *n.* An oval, yellow citrus fruit grown on a tree.

li·brar·y *n.* A collection of books, pamphlets, magazines, and reference books kept for reading.

light·ning *n.* The flash of light produced by a high-tension natural electric discharge into the atmosphere.

limb *n.* A large branch of a tree; an animal's appendage used for movement or grasping; an arm or leg.

lives *pl. n.* More than one life.

loaves *pl. n.* More than one loaf, such as a loaf of bread.

lo·cal *adj.* Pertaining to, being in, or serving a particular area or place.

lo·ca·tion *n.* A particular place.

lodge *n.* A house, such as a cabin, used as a temporary or seasonal dwelling.

lone·ly *adj.* Being without companions.

lug·gage *n.* Suitcases or other baggage used to carry items when traveling.

M

ma·chine *n.* A device or system built to use energy to do work.

man·age *v.* To direct or control the affairs or use of a place or event.

mean *v.* To have in mind as a purpose or intent. *adj.* Not nice. *n.* The average of a set of numbers.

meas·ure *v.* To determine the range, dimension, size, or capacity of anything.

me·di·an *n.* The middle number in a set of numbers arranged from least to greatest.

men·tion *v.* To refer to in passing or briefly.

mes·sage *n.* Any information, command, or news transmitted from one person to another.

met·al *n.* One of a category of hard solids, such as steel.

mice *pl. n.* Small rodents.

mild *adj.* Gentle in manner, behavior, or disposition; not severe or extreme.

mil·lion *n.* A number equal to 1,000 x 1,000.

min·er *n.* One who works underground in search of material, such as coal.

mi·nor *adj.* Not of legal age; lesser in degree, size, or importance.

mis·er·y *n.* A state of great unhappiness, distress, or pain.

mis·for·tune *n.* Bad luck or fortune.

mis·plac·ed *v.* Mislaid; put in a wrong place.

mis·print *n.* An error in a publication, such as a newspaper or book.

mis·quote *v.* To repeat incorrectly what someone has said.

mis·spell·ed *adj.* Not spelled right. *v.* Spelled a word wrongly.

mis·take *n.* An error; a wrong statement, action, or decision.

mod·el *n.* A small representation of an object.

mois·ture *n.* The presence of a small amount of liquid; dampness.

mo·ment *n.* A few seconds; a very short amount of time.

mon·key *n.* A member of the primates, excluding humans, having a long tail.

month·ly *adj.* Occurring, done, or payable each month.

mo·tion *n.* The act or process of changing position.

mo·tion·less *adj.* Not moving.

mo·tor *n.* A device that powers a machine.

mo·tor·cy·cle *n.* A two-wheeled vehicle powered by a motor.

moun·tain *n.* A land mass that rises above its surroundings and is higher than a hill.

mul·ti·ple *adj.* A number that is a product of a certain number and another number.

mus·cle *n.* Body tissue made of long cells that contract and produce movement.

mu·sic *n.* Pleasing or harmonious combinations of sounds.

N

nap·kin *n.* A cloth or soft paper, used while eating, for wiping the lips and fingers.

na·tion *n.* A group of people who are represented by one government.

nat·u·ral *adj.* Produced or existing by nature.

neigh·bor *n.* One who lives near another.

news·pa·per *n.* A weekly or daily publication that contains recent information.

nine·teen *n.* The number after eighteen and before twenty.

no·ble *adj.* Morally good.

nor·mal *adj.* Ordinary, average, usual.

note·book *n.* Sheets of paper bound together and used for writing.

no·tice *v.* To be aware of; to observe or pay attention to.

nu·mer·al *n.* A symbol or figure, or a group of these that represents a number.

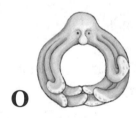

O

o·cean *n.* A huge body of salt water.

of·fice *n.* A place where people perform business or professional duties.

or·der *n.* A command. *v.* To command; to demand.

or·gan *n.* A part of an animal, human, or plant that performs a specific function.

o·ver *prep.* Above; across; upon.

oxen *pl. n.* Plural form of *ox*.

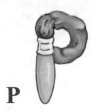

P

pack·age *n.* One or more items packed, wrapped, or bound together.

paint·ers' *poss. pl.* Belonging to people who paint.

palm *n.* The inner area of the hand between the fingers and the wrist.

pan·ic *n.* A sudden, uncontrollable fear. *v.* To be overcome by a sudden, uncontrollable fear.

pa·per *n.* A substance made of pulp from wood, used for writing upon.

par·ti·cle *n.* A very small piece of solid matter.

patch *n.* A piece of fabric used to repair a weakened or torn area in a garment.

peak *n.* The summit of a mountain; the top.

pearl *n.* A round, whitish gem formed inside an oyster.

peek *v.* To look at shyly or quickly, often from a place of hiding.

perch *n.* A place on which birds rest; any place for standing or sitting. *v.* To rest or sit upon.

per·fect *adj.* Having no defect or fault.

per·fect·ly *adv.* Having no defect or fault.

per·son *n.* A human being.

per·son·al·ly *adv.* In person; face to face.

pic·nic *n.* An outdoor social gathering with food.

pinch *v.* To squeeze between a finger and thumb, causing pain or discomfort.

plain *adj.* Ordinary; not rich or luxurious; not beautiful or highly decorated.

plas·tic *n.* A human-made material molded and then hardened into objects.

pleas·ure *n.* A feeling of satisfaction or enjoyment.

plunge *v.* To thrust or cast something, as into water.

pol·ish *v.* To make shiny and smooth by rubbing.

poor *adj.* Lacking possessions and money.

pore *n.* A tiny opening, as in the skin.

port *n.* A city or town with a harbor for loading and unloading cargo from ships.

por·trait *n.* A painting of a person.

pos·si·ble *adj.* Capable of being true, happening, or being accomplished.

pour *v.* To drop a liquid into another container.

pred·a·tor *n.* An animal that survives by eating other animals.

pret·ti·er *adj.* More attractive than others.

pret·ti·est *adj.* Most attractive of all.

pret·ty *adj.* Pleasant; attractive.

price *n.* The set amount of money expected or given for the sale of something; cost.

prism *n.* A solid figure with triangular ends and rectangular sides, used to disperse light into a spectrum.

pri·vate *adj.* Secluded or removed from the public view.

prob·a·bly *adv.* Most likely.

prod·uct *n.* Something produced, manufactured, or obtained.

prom·ise *n.* An assurance given that one will or will not do something; a pledge. *v.* To declare that one will or will not do something.

proof *n.* Evidence that supports a fact or shows that something is true.

pro·pose *v.* To present or put forward for consideration or action.

pro·tec·tion *n.* Something that shields a person, animal, or thing from harm; the act of keeping safe from harm.

pro·ton *n.* An atomic particle with a positive charge.

pub·lish *v.* To print and distribute books, magazines, or newspapers to the public.

punch *n.* A drink made from different substances, often fruit juice. *v.* To hit sharply with the hand or fist.

pur·pose *n.* A desired goal; an intention.

puz·zle *n.* A mystery or riddle. *v.* To bewilder; to confuse.

Q

ques·tion *n.* An expression of inquiry that requires an answer. *v.* To ask.

quite *adv.* To the fullest degree; really; actually; to a great extent.

R

rack·et *n.* An instrument used to play tennis.

ra·di·us *n.* A line from the center of a circle to its surface.

ranch *n.* A large establishment for raising cattle, sheep, or other livestock.

range *n.* The limits between which something varies or changes; a tract of land over which animals such as cattle and horses graze.

rap·id·ly *adv.* With great speed.

rat·tle·snake *n.* A poisonous reptile with segments at the end of its tail that make a rattling sound.

re·act *v.* To act in response to.

reason *n.* The explanation for doing something.

re·cent·ly *adv.* In the near past; not long ago.

rec·og·nize *v.* To experience or identify something or someone as having been known previously.

re·cord *v.* To write down for future use or permanent reference.

re·cy·cle *v.* To make suitable for reuse.

re·fuse *v.* To decline or reject; to strongly state unwillingness to do something.

re·gret *v.* To feel disappointed or sorry about.

reg·u·lar *adj.* Usual; normal; conforming to a set of principles or procedures.

re·ject *v.* To refuse to accept.

re·mem·ber *v.* To bring back or recall to the mind.

re·move *v.* To take off or away; to get rid of.

re·peat *v.* To do again.

re·port *n.* A detailed account about observations. *v.* To give a detailed account or statement.

re·spect·ful *adv.* Full of consideration or courtesy for.

rest·less *adv.* Nervous; unable to rest.

re·treat *n.* A place where one can rest and relax; the act of withdrawing from danger. *v.* To withdraw, as from battle.

re·turn *v.* To come back to an earlier place or condition.

re·view *v.* To study or look over something again.

ri·ver *n.* A large stream.

ro·tate *v.* To turn on an axis.

roy·al *adj.* Relating to a king or queen.

S

safe·ly *adv.* In a way without danger.

sal·ad *n.* A dish usually made of green vegetables, fruit, or meat tossed with dressing.

sand·wich *n.* Two or more slices of bread with a filling, such as cheese or meat, placed between them.

scale *n.* A device for weighing; a flat plate that covers certain animals, especially fish and reptiles.

scarves *pl. n.* Wide pieces of cloth used to keep the neck warm.

scent *n.* A smell; an odor.

sci·ence *n.* The study and explanation of things and events in nature and in the universe.

scram·ble *v.* To move with panic.

scrap·book *n.* A book for collecting photos, various paper items, or other flat objects.

scrape *n.* a mark left on a surface by the rubbing of something against it; a minor cut on the skin. *v.* To rub or move roughly along a surface.

scream *n.* A sharp cry of fear or pain. *v.* To utter a long, sharp cry, as of fear or pain.

screech *v.* To make a shrill, harsh noise.

screw *n.* A metal piece that resembles a nail, having a spiral thread used for fastening things together.

scrib·ble *v.* To write without thought or care to penmanship.

search *v.* To try to find something.

se·cret·ly *adv.* In a hidden or mysterious manner.

select *v.* To choose or pick out.

sen·tence *n.* A series of words arranged to express a complete thought.

sep·a·rate *adj.* Apart from others.

set·tle *v.* To colonize; to adjust or place in a proper position; to make quiet or calm.

se·ven·teen *n.* The number after sixteen and before eighteen.

sheep *n.* A herding mammal with thick, wooly fur.

shel·ter *n.* Something that gives protection or cover.

shel·ves *pl. n.* Surfaces for storing objects, such as books or dishes.

shield *n.* A piece of protective metal or wood held in front of the body. *v.* To protect.

shift *n.* A period of working. *v.* To change direction or position.

shirt *n.* A garment worn on the upper part of the body.

side·line *n.* The edge of a court or sports field that marks its limits.

sight *n.* The ability to see with the eyes; an image seen with the eyes.

signal *n.* An action or symbol that warns, directs, or informs. *v.* To make a sign of warning or instruction.

si·lent *adj.* Making no sound.

sim·ple *adj.* Easy to do or understand.

site *n.* A location, as of a city, building, or historical event.

six·teen *n.* The number after fifteen and before seventeen.

skate·board *n.* A narrow piece of wood with wheels attached for a person to move along a concrete surface.

sketch *n.* A rough drawing or outline. *v.* To make a rough drawing or outline.

slight *adj.* Minor; unimportant.

smooth *adj.* Having an even surface; flat; without irregularity.

snatch *v.* To seize or grasp something suddenly.

sock·et *n.* A hollow opening into which something is fitted; an electrical outlet.

sol·id *adj.* Having a definite, firm shape and volume. *n.* A three-dimensional figure.

sol·u·tion *n.* An answer to a problem; a combination of liquids.

some·where *n.* An unspecified place.

sor·ry *adj.* Feeling or showing sympathy or regret.

source *n.* Any point of origin or beginning.

spark·le *v.* To give off light.

special *adj.* Unusual, exceptional, or uncommon.

spe·cies *n.* A group of animals or plants that share the same characteristics and can mate with other members of the same species.

spoke *n.* One of the rods that serve to connect and support the rim of a wheel. *v.* Past tense of *speak*; talked.

spot·less *adj.* Perfectly clean; without flaws.

squash *n.* An edible fruit of the gourd family. *v.* To press or squeeze into a soft pulp.

squeak·y *adj.* Having a sharp, penetrating sound.

squid *n.* A type of ten-armed marine animal with a tapered body.

squirm *v.* To twist the body in a wiggling motion.

stat·ue *n.* A form sculpted from wood, clay, metal, or stone.

steak *n.* A piece of meat, usually from a cow, cooked and eaten.

steam *n.* Water in the form of vapor, caused by heat.

stew *n.* A mixture of food, usually meat and vegetables, cooked on low heat for a long period of time. *v.* To cook slowly; to simmer; to boil.

stom·ach *n.* The organ of the body into which food passes from the esophagus to begin the process of digestion; belly, abdomen.

stop·light *n.* A signalling device that controls the flow of automobile traffic at intersections.

strap *n.* A long, narrow strip of leather or other material used to secure objects.

straw *n.* A stalk of dried, threshed grain; a slender, plastic or paper tube used to suck up a liquid.

streak *n.* A line or mark that is a different color from the surrounding area.

strength *n.* The quality of being strong.

stretch *v.* To extend fully.

string *n.* A strip of thin twine or wire.

sud·den *adj.* Happening very quickly without warning or notice.

sug·gest *v.* To give an idea for action or consideration.

suit *n.* A set of clothes to be worn together.

sun·nier *adj.* Having more sunlight than other places.

sun·niest *adj.* Having the most sunlight of all places.

sup·ply *v.* To provide with what is needed; to make available.

sup·port *v.* To bear or hold the weight of.

sure *adj.* Certain; being impossible to doubt.

sur·face *n.* The exterior or outside boundary of something.

surge *v.* To increase suddenly. *n.* A burst, as of water or energy.

surprise *v.* To startle.

swal·low *v.* To cause food to pass from the mouth to the stomach.

sweet *adj.* Having a sugary, agreeable flavor.

sym·bol *n.* Something that stands for or represents something else.

T

ta·ble *n.* An article of furniture having a flat top, supported by legs.

tem·per·a·ture *n.* A measure of heat or cold in relation to the body or environment.

ter·ri·ble *adj.* Horrible; causing fear or terror.

thank·ful *adj.* Grateful; feeling or showing gratitude.

them·selves *pron.* Them or they.

thieves *pl. n.* People who steal; robbers.

thirst·y *adj.* Having a need or desire for a drink of water or other refreshing liquid.

thir·teen *n.* The number after twelve and before fourteen.

thirty *n.* The number after twenty-nine and before thirty-one.

thought·ful *adj.* Showing care or consideration for another; engaged in thinking.

threat *n.* An expression or warning of harm.

thrill *n.* A feeling of sudden, intense excitement, fear, or joy.

throat *n.* The front section or part of the neck containing passages for food and air.

throne *n.* The chair on which a ruler sits.

through *prep.* From the beginning to the end; in one side and out the other; by means of.

throw *v.* To toss or fling through the air.

tick·et *n.* A printed slip of paper or cardboard allowing its holder to enter a specified event or to enjoy a privilege.

tide *n.* The rise and fall of the surface level of the ocean.

ti·tle *n.* An identifying name of a book, poem, play, or other creative work; a word used with a person's name to show respect, a profession, or rank.

tomb *n.* A vault for burying the dead; a grave.

to·tal·ly *adv.* Completely.

touch *n.* The sense by which objects are observed by contact with the skin. *v.* To allow a part of the body, as the hands, to feel something else; to come in contact with.

tow·el *n.* An absorbent piece of cloth used for drying or wiping.

traf·fic *n.* The passage or movement of vehicles.

trav·el *v.* To journey or move from one place to another.

treat *n.* A pleasant surprise. *v.* To behave or act toward.

trem·ble *v.* To shake, as with fear or from cold.

trick·le *n.* A small stream, as of water. *v.* To flow in droplets or a small stream.

troop *n.* A group or assembly of people.

trop·ic·al *adj.* Being hot and humid in climate.

trou·ble *n.* Difficulty or danger; something that causes a problem.

truce *n.* A temporary end to fighting or a disagreement.

tru·ly *adj.* Really, actually; certainly.

twelve *n.* The number after eleven and before thirteen.

twenty *n.* The number after nineteen and before twenty-one.

twitch *v.* To move or cause to move in a jerky manner.

U

ug·li·er *adj.* More unpleasant to look at than others.

ug·li·est *adj.* Most unpleasant to look at than all others.

ug·ly *adj.* Offensive or unpleasant to look at.

um·brel·la *n.* A collapsible frame covered with plastic or cloth, held above the head as protection from sun or rain.

un·a·ble *adj.* Not having the necessary capabilities, skills, or power.

un·a·ware *adj.* Not realizing.

un·earth *v.* To discover; to dig up.

un·fair *adj.* Not just; not following accepted rules.

u·ni·form *n.* Identical clothing worn by the members of a group.

u·ni·ty *n.* The fact or state of being one.

un·less *conj.* Only with the condition that something else happens.

un·til *prep.* Up to the time of.

up·per *adj.* Higher in status, position, or location.

u·su·al·ly *adv.* Happening regularly or often.

V

va·ca·tion *n.* A period of time away from work for pleasure, relaxation, or rest.

val·ley *n.* Low land between ranges of hills or mountains.

val·ue *n.* The worth or cost of something. *v.* To appreciate or consider as being important.

vi·ta·min *n.* Any of various substances found in foods that are essential to good health.

vol·can·o *n.* A mountain through which lava is forced out.

W

waist *n.* The narrow part of the body between the chest and hips.

waste *n.* Worthless material or trash; the act of carelessly using up something. *v.* To use up carelessly.

wa·ter *n.* The clear liquid making up oceans, lakes, and streams.

wa·ter·fall *n.* A flowing body of water, such as a river or stream, falling from a height.

weath·er *n.* The condition of the air or atmosphere in terms of humidity, temperature, and similar features.

week·ly *adv.* Once a week.

weight *n.* The amount of heaviness of something.

whose *pron.* Belonging to or having to do with one's belongings.

win·dow *n.* An opening built into a wall for light and air; a pane of glass.

wise·ly *adv.* In an intelligent manner.

wives *pl. n.* Married women.

wolves *pl. n.* More than one wolf.

won·der·ful *adj.* Very good or excellent; causing amazement.

wor·ry *v.* To be concerned or troubled.

worth·less *adj.* Having no worth or value.

wreath *n.* A decorative, ringlike form of intertwined flowers, bows, and other articles.

wreck *v.* To crash into something; to ruin.

wren *n.* A small, brown songbird.

wrench *n.* A tool used to secure bolts.

wrin·kle *n.* A small crease on the skin or on fabric.

Y

young *adj.* Of or relating to the early stage of life; not old.

Parts of Speech

adj. = adjective
adv. = adverb
art. = article
conj. = conjunction
n. = noun
prep. = preposition
pron. = pronoun
v. = verb

Answer Key

Say each word. Listen for the short **a** sound and the short **e** sound. Then, write the word.

Spelling Tip	The short **a** and short **e** sounds often come between two consonants. The symbol for the short **a** sound is /a/. The symbol for the short **e** sound is /e/.

Spelling Words

sandwich	sandwich
blanket	blanket
effort	effort
package	package
extra	extra
traffic	traffic
napkin	napkin
panic	panic
basket	basket
address	address
cabin	cabin
banner	banner
gather	gather
salad	salad
celery	celery

6

Words in Context

Write the missing spelling words.

Challenge
Circle the other two-syllable words in the narrative with the /a/ and /e/ sounds.

Rest from the City

Last weekend my family stayed at a **cabin** in the woods. First, we all had to make an **effort** to **gather** up the things we needed to take. We loaded all our bags and a large **package** of supplies into the car. As we left the busy streets of the city crowded with **traffic**, we began to relax.

Once we got into the country, we started looking for the **address** of our cabin on the mailboxes near the road. There was a moment of **panic** when we thought we were lost. Then, my dad saw the large red **banner** with the name of our campground written on it. We had finally arrived.

After we unpacked our things, we decided to go on a picnic. My mom packed a **basket** full of food and covered it with a large **napkin**. My brother and I found a shady spot and spread out a **blanket** to sit on. We each had a ham **sandwich** with **extra** lettuce and tomato. We also had a mixed fruit **salad** and crisp stalks of **celery** spread with peanut butter. After we ate, we took a walk through the woods.

7

Fun with Words

Unscramble the letters to make spelling words. Then, unscramble the letters that you circle to solve the riddle.

1. frictaf _____ traffic _____ Circle letters 2 and 6.
2. creyle _____ celery _____ Circle letters 3 and 6.
3. banic _____ cabin _____ Circle letter 1.
4. pankni _____ napkin _____ Circle letter 1.
5. takbes _____ basket _____ Circle letter 6.
6. daserds _____ address _____ Circle letters 4 and 5.
7. eakgcap _____ package _____ Circle letter 3.
8. trofef _____ effort _____ Circle letter 4.

What word in the dictionary is spelled incorrectly? **incorrectly**

Words Across the Curriculum

Say each science word. Then, write the word.

1. cactus **cactus**
2. desert **desert**
3. element **element**
4. predator **predator**

Write the missing science words.

A **desert** is a hot, dry habitat that is home to many plants and animals. The dominant type of plant in this habitat is the **cactus**. A common **predator** that eats small lizards and mice in this habitat is the rattlesnake. In the American Southwest, the **element** silver is found under the layers of sand and rock.

8

Words in Writing

Write a narrative about something you like to do with your family. Use at least four words from the box.

Answers will vary.

sandwich	package	napkin	address	gather	cactus	desert
blanket	extra	panic	cabin	salad	element	predator
effort	traffic	basket	banner	celery		

Misspelled Words

Read the narrative and circle the seven misspelled words. Then, write the words correctly on the lines below.

I like to help my dad gather vegetables from the garden. I pull carrots and celery from the ground and put them in a basket. I also pick tomatoes, peppers, and other vegetables to use in a salad or on a sandwich. Taking care of a garden is hard work, but it's worth the extra effort.

gather	basket	sandwich	effort
celery	salad	extra	

9

Notes

Notes

Notes

Notes

Notes

Notes

Notes

Notes

Notes

Notes

Notes

Notes